CHRISTINE DE PIZAN

Covering one of the most fascinating yet misunderstood periods in history, the MEDIEVAL LIVES series presents medieval people, concepts and events, drawing on political and social history, philosophy, material culture (art, architecture and archaeology) and the history of science. These books are global and wide-ranging in scope, encompassing both Western and non-Western subjects, and span the fifth to the fifteenth centuries, tracing significant developments from the collapse of the Roman Empire onwards.

SERIES EDITOR: Deirdre Jackson

Christine de Pizan: Life, Work, Legacy *Charlotte Cooper-Davis*

Margery Kempe: A Mixed Life *Anthony Bale*

CHRISTINE DE PIZAN

Life, Work, Legacy

CHARLOTTE COOPER-DAVIS

REAKTION BOOKS

For dad, in memoriam
and for Alistair, in anticipation

Published by Reaktion Books Ltd
Unit 32, Waterside
44–48 Wharf Road
London N1 7UX, UK
www.reaktionbooks.co.uk

First published 2021
Copyright © Charlotte Cooper-Davis 2021

Printed and bound in India by Replika Press Pvt. Ltd

A catalogue record for this book is available from the British Library

ISBN 978 1 78914 442 0

CONTENTS

Introduction

Oh . . . you have done me a great favor by taking me to Long
Study, for I am fated to practice it for my entire life.
Le Livre du chemin de long estude[1]

ew medieval writers were as prolific as Christine de Pizan.
Over a career that spanned almost four decades, she
composed around thirty major works as well as several
shorter poems. These survive in over two hundred manuscripts
– an extraordinary figure for an individual medieval author. For
comparison, just a single manuscript exists of the Old English
epic poem *Beowulf* and even Chaucer's *Canterbury Tales*, which
were being composed around the time that Christine was writing, survive in only 32 copies. What is even more remarkable
in Christine's case is that she oversaw the production of 54 of
her manuscripts herself and several of them are written in her
own hand. It is not known how many further copies of her works
are likely to have been lost over the centuries.

Such an enormous literary production would not have been
possible had its executor not been deeply familiar with contemporary culture and compositional practices. For her works to
circulate, a pragmatic knowledge of writing, bookmaking and

Miniature of Fortune spinning her wheel, taking some men down and
making others greater, from *Collected Works* (The Book of the Queen),
c. 1410–14.

booktrading was required; for them to be popular, they needed to display a mastery of popular and fashionable poetic themes, which would also secure her valuable patronage from some of the highest-ranking nobles of the time. Gaining the dexterity required to be proficient in these various areas was no easy task in the Middle Ages – especially for a woman without a clerical education – so despite her prolific output, Christine did not turn to writing until relatively late in life. Before she was to take up her pen, her life was to undergo a series of twists and turns that would set her on the path to becoming an author.

Christine was born in Venice around 1364, but she only spent a short amount of time in that city. Her father, Thomas de Pizan – Thomasso de Benvenuto da Pizzano, to give him his full Italian name – was appointed astrologer to the French court in Paris shortly before 1368. Once he had settled in the city, he sent for his family to join him. It was through her father and his position that Christine first became embedded in the literary and scholastic culture of the late European Middle Ages. When she was born, Thomas was a lecturer at the prestigious Italian University of Bologna, which he had also attended as a student and where he was a contemporary of the poet and scholar Petrarch. The education that he received would have been second to none. He trained to become a doctor in medical studies, which required studying the arts along with astrology and natural philosophy, mathematics, logic and rhetoric.[2] In her writings, Christine remembers her father with great fondness as someone who was 'famous everywhere as a celebrated scholar', from whom she humbly claims to have gathered only 'the crumbs falling from the high table ... when fine dishes are served up'.[3] She describes how Thomas encouraged her in her own learning and did not see her sex as an obstacle to erudition. As one of the characters in *Le Livre de la cité des dames* (The Book of the City of Ladies) reminds her: 'he was delighted to see your passion for study.'[4]

A love of learning ran in the family. This was probably what drew Thomas to accept the position at the French court, which was famous for its intellectual culture (he turned down a similar role he had been offered at the court of Hungary when forced to choose between the two). King Charles v of France, who came to the throne around the same time that Christine was born, was a monarch committed to learning. He had recently embarked upon a huge enterprise, known as his *Sapientia* (meaning 'knowledge') project, which involved investing heavily in new books that would be housed in a sumptuous new library in the Louvre. To do so, he commissioned numerous writers and artisans to fill his shelves with new works – these were not only literary works, but testaments to the various forms of cultural and artistic practices that were thriving in Paris at the time. Charles v's project did not just require authors and scribes to compose and copy the texts, but the work of translators, illuminators and artists, bookmakers, carpenters and metalworkers, architects and designers. Meanwhile, the flourishing University of Paris (of which Charles was a patron) continued to attract leading scholars to the city, many of whom went on to take up positions at the royal court. Through her father's work, Christine would get to know many of the people who carried out these duties in a personal capacity.

This thriving intellectual and artistic atmosphere formed the backdrop to Christine's youth. Without the benefit of such a rich cultural background or her father's connections, she might not have had access to the materials that enabled her career as a writer to take shape. Yet, although she undoubtedly enjoyed a period of great happiness, the circumstances that led her to take on this role are hardly enviable.

At Fortune's Mercy

When she was fifteen years old, Christine married a royal secretary named Etienne de Castel, who was about ten years her senior. Like her father, Etienne was university-educated, and Christine describes her admiration for his great learning in similar terms to those she expresses for her father. Although her husband was chosen by Thomas, there is no reason to believe the union was anything but happy. Christine herself concedes that 'truly . . . I would not have essayed to choose better by my own wishes.'[5] She often refers to her eleven-year marriage in her writings, where her husband is mentioned only with fondness. In the autobiographical passages of *Le Livre de la mutacion de Fortune* (The Book of Fortune's Transformation) he is described as 'a handsome, pleasing youth' whose company she enjoyed and who 'was so faithful to me, and so good that . . . I could not praise highly enough the good things that I received from him.'[6] She and Etienne had three children together, two of whom survived. One of them, Jean de Castel, also went on to have a career as a writer. The decade of Christine's life during which she was married was a happy and prosperous time for her and her family.

Alas, it was not to last. Between 1380 and 1390 Christine was dealt a series of blows, starting with the death of Charles v, who – as employer to both her husband and father – was her family's main protector. Etienne and Thomas's financial situations both suffered as a result. In *Le Livre de l'avision Cristine* (The Book of Christine's Vision), the third part of which is largely autobiographical, she describes the effects of the king's death on her father's income, including his loss of pensions and other benefits. It is unclear how long Thomas outlived his protector, but he is believed to have died sometime in the late 1380s. Christine has recourse to a common metaphor to relate the tragedies that afflicted her at this time – that of the wheel of Fortune. Up until now, she says, Fortune had smiled on her, provided for her and looked after her, but now she had 'placed me in the downward swing of her wheel, set towards the misfortunes she wished to give me to throw me as low as possible'.[7] The final turn of Fortune's wheel came in 1390. Etienne was with the new king on a mission in Beauvais when an epidemic struck. He did not survive the outbreak. Etienne's death left Christine widowed in her mid-twenties,with three children, a mother and a niece to feed.

Christine's life was transformed as she was left to fend for her young family. But although her finances suffered immensely with the deaths of the family's two main earners, her position could have been much worse. At the height of his power, Thomas had earned a very good income – estimated at around 1,920 *livres parisis* (the main currency in which accounts were paid in Paris at that time) per annum. At the time, the income of even the middle nobility was only around a quarter of that amount.[8] Although the family's finances suffered enormously, their background was sufficiently wealthy for the effects of these events not to be entirely devastating. Christine and her two brothers, who by now were back in Italy, inherited property from their father both in France and in their native land. Thomas's property in Melun was later sold by Christine to an old friend of the family's, the author Philippe de Mézières – himself a minor noble and just one of the family's many important connections. As for Etienne's estate, for fourteen years Christine fought various lawsuits that would release her from responsibility for her husband's property. The details of these lawsuits are unknown but it is probably the case that Christine was being forced to pay rent on Etienne's property even though it had reverted to the crown upon his death.[9] Meanwhile, the debtors who owed money to the estate avoided and eluded her. Christine speaks candidly of her economic difficulties in the *Avision*, but it is important to remember that she was never so desperate as to be forced to work or to remarry – as was so often the case for upper-class widows in the Middle Ages. She did need to support her family, however, and to justify and ensure their continued presence at court by maintaining the powerful connections that her husband and father had fostered. And so, she turned to writing.

In the *Mutacion*, Christine's obligation to provide for her household is described as a dramatic transformation – one in which she is reborn a man. In this part of the narrative, she recounts her marriage through the allegory of a sea voyage. A man named Hymen (who as part of the allegory stands for marriage itself) places her in a ship of which her husband is the captain. Soon, the boat hits rough seas and he is thrown overboard. Following this, Christine (or, more accurately, the protagonist who – as is frequently the case in her works – bears her name) enters a period of profound devastation and mourning, until Fortune once again intervenes. Christine describes how Fortune 'touched me all over my body; she palpated and took in her hands each bodily part'. When she awoke, she found herself transformed:

> I felt my limbs to be stronger than before, and the great
> pain and lamentation which had earlier dominated me,
> I felt to be somewhat lessened . . . Then I felt myself much
> lighter than usual and I felt that my flesh was changed and
> strengthened, and my voice much lowered, and my body
> harder and faster . . . I felt that I had become a true man.[10]

Christine, reborn a man, surveys her damaged vessel. Seeing that it has already taken on a great deal of water and is in danger of sinking, she sets about repairing it. She plugs the holes, repairs the wood, bails out the hold, and is soon able to navigate the ship with confidence. Writing in 1403, she says she has now been a man for thirteen years, and will continue to be such from now on. The gender-transformation aspect of the *Mutacion* has attracted much attention over the years. Though Christine is referring to the role that she took on as head of the family, as opposed to any biological transformation, because 'being a man or a woman was already recognized in . . . the Middle Ages as a gendered role that was not determined by biological sex', it is possible that Christine took her gender transformation quite literally.[11]

Christine mending her ship can be understood as her tending to and looking after her family by assuming her new role as head of the household and its principal (if not sole) earner. Few exact details concerning the financial reward Christine received for her writings have survived, but there are some archival references to payments made to her from certain patrons.[12] Artisans who were paid were typically housed by their patrons too, so it is likely that Christine offered her books to those who sheltered and protected her family. Exchanges between artists and patrons often took place within complex networks of gift-giving where protection and housing were compensated with artistic gifts, and vice versa.[13]

The hands-on nature of the repairs that Christine is described as carrying out to her vessel in the *Mutacion* also mirrors the practical tasks she began to carry out in her role as a professional writer: composing, writing and compiling books – an aspect of her involvement in contemporary artistic production that will be delved into further on in this book. Her increasing confidence in steering the ship also metaphorically conveys the greater confidence she gained as a writer: after first undertaking small tasks and simple repairs to the boat (representing her shorter early poetic works), she soon acquired the confidence to rival the more substantial works being produced by her peers. Having clung to the spokes of Fortune's wheel, Christine de Pizan was reborn as a professional writer.

The Beginnings of a Writing Career

Christine dates her literary debut to 1399, nine years into her widowhood, although some of her poems, such as the ninth in her collection *Les Cent balades* (One Hundred Ballades),were written before then.[14] In terms of their form and the topics they broach, Christine's writings are in many ways typical of her times. Her earliest compositions followed the poetic set forms of the period: ballades (a set-form poem that consisted of three stanzas followed by an envoy), of which almost three hundred of hers have survived, as well as lays, virelays and roundels – popular set-form poems of the period. These popular forms of lyric poetry were frequently born out of games, competitions and collaboration. Individuals from the households of the French royal princes composed and recited their poetic creations at assemblies such as the *cour amoureuse* (amorous court), which met several times throughout the year. Among its members were princes from the highest ranks of the nobility, intellectuals from the upper bourgeoisie, courtiers who held administrative functions, as well as professional poets and writers. Fixed-form poems were submitted to these gatherings and judged according to their rhetorical merits.[15] Another kind of game that took place at court consisted of poetic exchanges in which someone would put forward a single line of verse to which the rest of the assembly would then compose responses.[16] Writing poetry of the kind that Christine composed therefore required its authors to be actively engaged in collaborative forms of cultural production and to understand the rules that governed poetic composition. It is not certain that Christine took part in any such competitions, or if she was ever a member of gatherings such as the *cour amoureuse*, but the form of some of her earliest poetry is in keeping with the kinds of works that were submitted at these events. The title of one of her first

collections of poetry, *Les Jeux a vendre* (Games for Sale), which
is made up of seventy short response verses and whose title
recalls a particular type of poetic game called the 'venditions',
indicates that she was no stranger to this courtly creative
practice.

Christine's early poetry draws on many themes that were popular among her contemporaries. Love, a perennial theme in the
late Middle Ages, takes pride of place in Christine's lyric poetry,
where she writes in both the female and male voice. She also
reflects the contemporary fashion for classical themes, populating
her poetry with figures such as the goddesses Juno, Minerva, Pallas
and Venus or the great heroes of classical mythology – Paris and
Helen, Hero and Leander. A large amount of medieval poetry was
devotional, as witnessed in several of Christine's verses, including *La Passion de Jhesu nostre sauveur* (The Passion of Jesus Our
Saviour) and *L'Oroyson Nostre Dame* (A Prayer to Our Lady),
composed in honour of the Virgin Mary. Christine was later to
treat her earlier works as light and somewhat frivolous compared
to the more serious works she produced later on in her career.
Yet, although some of them are short and relatively playful, as is
often the nature of poetry produced for poetic games, there is frequently a moralizing, didactic tone to her poetry. Her *Proverbes
moraux* (Moral Proverbs), for instance, consist of 101 couplets
proffering advice on good conduct, an aim that is shared by her
Enseignements moraux (Moral Teachings), which are addressed
to her son. Other lyrical verses, such as ballades 58 and 64 of her
Cent balades, offer advice to knights on good conduct. In ballade 43 of her *Autres balades* (Other Ballades) she warns against
false lovers, counselling women of honour not to believe the
deceitful flattery of men who pretend to be respectful, but who
actually set out to defame them – a theme on which she expands
in some of her longer poetic compositions. In presenting this
advice, Christine frequently advises her readers to trust in three

sources: ancient philosophers, those she simply terms 'the wise' (often indicating scholars at court, which would have counted her father), and God. A final source of inspiration came in the form of current events. Several of Christine's texts engage directly with contemporary political matters at length, although even some of her shortest compositions allow her to discuss significant events: take, for instance, the moving ballade that she addressed to the royal family on the death of the Duke of Burgundy in 1404 (*Autres balades*, 42).

Later in her career, Christine rather modestly ascribed some of her success as a poet to the novelty of her being a woman writer. This may be true in part, but her poetic skill rivalled that of many contemporaries, including the influential and prolific writers Alain Chartier, Eustache Deschamps and Jean Froissart. Because they composed lyric poetry in set forms, these poets operated in a system of shared literary conventions in which they borrowed from and imitated each other's work. Part of the individual poet's challenge was to push the boundaries of these set forms, composing poetry that followed the formal constraints (in terms of rhyme patterns, number of lines and so on), but innovated creatively within their limits. Regardless of her sex, Christine was a firm member of this coterie of court poets.

In addition to writing on popular topics, Christine drew heavily on her own life experience, especially her widowhood. 'I am a widow, alone, and dressed in black,' opens the third of her roundels.[17] In fact, it is in what is often termed her 'personal poetry', where she uses autobiographical details to create a sympathetic poetic persona, that she distinguishes herself most notably from her contemporaries. It is also here that she is most inventive in her use of fixed-form conventions. Perhaps her most famous poem, ballade 11 of her *Cent balades*, is remarkable for its striking patterns of repetition and sparse use of language. The first stanza suffices to give a sense of its tone:

Alone am I and alone I wish to be,
Alone my gentle love has left me;
Alone am I, without companion or master,
Alone am I, sorrowful and vexed;
Alone am I in anxious weariness;
Alone am I, more lost than any other;
Alone am I, left without a lover.[18]

The repetition of 'alone' at the start of each of the poem's 25 lines and the juxtaposition of contrasting emotions (sorrowful and vexed; anxious and weary) contribute towards a moving, mournful effect that is unique and memorable.

The classical themes, moral and instructive aims, devotional content, autobiographic details and 'pro-feminine' (that is, pro-women) messages seen in her very earliest poetry continue to feature in the longer works that she began to compose from around 1402. Although she soon moved away from composing collections of lyric poetry and began to write in prose, she never stopped writing in verse. Her first autobiographical work is *Le Livre du chemin de long estude* (The Book of the Path of Long Study), another verse narrative that allegorically describes her path to becoming a scholar. She draws on her life experience again in the prose *Cité des dames*, which is best known as her major pro-feminine treatise. Its sequel, *Le Livre des trois vertus* (The Book of the Three Virtues), offers women practical advice on how to conduct themselves and manage their households. Verse, prose, classical, didactic and devotional themes are combined in her *L'Epistre Othea* (The Epistle of Othea), which draws on details from classical mythology to instruct a prince on good behaviour, ending with a reminder that the Bible itself shows the utility of a woman's teachings. This last work comprises 101 miniatures, many of which were created especially for the *Othea*, thereby illustrating a more practical aspect of Christine's cultural enterprise: in order to produce such a manuscript, she would have worked closely with the miniaturists who carried out the illuminations for her texts.

Her poetic skill earned Christine a reputation as a writer and brought her to the attention of several of the highest members of the nobility, who went on to become her patrons. These included Charles v's brother Philip, Duke of Burgundy; his son, Louis of Orleans; and the Queen of France, Isabeau of Bavaria. Christine does not stop short of praising her patrons for their financial support. For example, in a memorable passage of the *Avision*, she recounts the assistance Philip of Burgundy gave in exchange for copies of her works and praises him for extending his generosity to her son, whom he also employed.[19]

A Politically Engaged Writer

No overview of Christine's literary output would be complete without mentioning her political writings, which present a substantial body of works. One of the texts that contributed towards Christine's enduring reputation after her death is her biography of Charles v, *Le Livre des fais et bonnes meurs du sage roy Charles v* (The Book of the Deeds and Good Conduct of the Wise King Charles v), which was commissioned by Philip of Burgundy. This book is a homage to the enormous cultural capital that Charles had brought to the French kingdom and a celebration of his great learning. She also composed two practical manuals on good governance, *Le Livre du corps de policie* (The Book of the Body Politic), and on military conduct, *Le Livre des fais d'armes et de chevalerie* (The Book of Deeds of Arms and of Chivalry). Despite the military strain of some of these titles, Christine was above all a pacifist. She begged her readers to help bring to an end the wars that were currently afflicting France. Her *Lamentacions sur les maux de la France* (Lamentation on France's Ills) and *Livre de la paix* (Book of Peace) engage directly with the effects on the

French population of the civil war and of the Hundred Years War, which were unfolding around her. As its name suggests, her *Epistre a la reine de France* (Epistle to the Queen of France) is a direct address to the queen, whom Christine begs to intervene to help spare France and its people.

The beginning and the end of Christine's life are both marked by a journey. The long voyage that she undertook as a child from Venice to Paris is the first event recounted in the *Avision*. In contrast, her departure from Paris in 1418 at the height of wartime brutalities is not described in her writings. Her pen, which had been so active for the previous 25 years, abruptly fell silent. In the last decade of her life, she composed only two works. The first, *Les Heures de contemplation de la Passion* (Contemplation on the Passion of Our Lord), is a devotional work, probably intended for the use of the nuns at the convent where she was in hiding. For a long time, this was believed to be the abbey of Poissy, where her daughter was a nun.[20] *Le Ditié Jehanne d'Arc* (The Tale of Joan of Arc), composed in 1429, is her final work. For the modern reader, who hardly needs to be told of Joan of Arc's tragic fate, there is an extremely bitter irony to the enraptured tone of Christine's poem, which celebrates her rise. In its opening lines, she tells us that, after eleven long years spent weeping in an abbey, 'I begin now for the first time to laugh' and 'I will change my language from weeping into singing.' The reason for her joy? 'That God has wished to bestow His grace on France . . . through a tender virgin'.[21] For Christine, Joan had been sent by God to bring about French victory against the English. But her source of joy was not simply that much-needed help had finally arrived, it was that that help took on a female form. Christine herself can scarcely believe it:

Oh, what an honor to the female sex! That God loves it is clear with all these wretched people and traitors who laid

waste the whole kingdom cast out and the realm elevated
and restored by a woman – something a hundred thousand
men could not have done! Before, one would not have
believed it possible.[22]

Christine's eager hopes for Joan – that she would take back
Paris from the English and end her life having conquered the
Holy Land – were never to be fulfilled. Nothing further is known
of Christine's fate after composing the *Ditié*, although we can
only hope that she did not live to see her heroine's downfall and
capture in 1430, or her burning at the stake the following year.
With the *Ditié*, Christine's engagement with her political landscape endured to the end. Her hopes that Joan would take back
Paris would mean that she could, at long last, return to the city
that, even after over a decade in enforced hiding, she still
thought of as home – a hope that was never fulfilled.

Throughout her life and in all of her works, Christine was
an active participant in her cultural environment. That is to say,
the artistic and compositional practices of the period, its the-
matic conventions and the contemporary political sphere. For
material, Christine drew heavily on literary sources from the
past and her legacy has been to have an impact on artistic production many centuries after her death. As such, she is an author
who is engaged with her cultural past, present and future. The
chapters that follow explore each of these aspects of Christine's
cultural engagement in turn, starting with her cultural present.
As mentioned, Christine's writings should be situated alongside
the literature being composed by her peers, since they had such
a significant influence on her own works, but in producing a
large number of her own manuscripts, she also went further
than any other late medieval author by taking an active role
in the manufacture of her works. After exploring the various
cultural and political activities that were taking place in her

contemporary Paris in Chapter One, this practical aspect to Christine's literary work forms the subject of Chapter Two, where we delve into her involvement in the thriving Parisian artistic scene. In Chapter Three, we then take a deeper look at some of Christine's texts themselves and how they were composed – in particular, her handling of literary sources. It was not unusual at the time in which she was writing to draw heavily on the works of previous authors, but this practice often led to the recycling of nefarious views – something she calls out in what are now often termed her pro-feminine writings. Although Christine also relied on other works for inspiration, she shows the risks involved in using them unthinkingly, especially in terms of perpetrating misogynous claims against women. In the final chapter, we turn to Christine's legacy and to an aspect of her participation in cultural creations that she cannot have anticipated: her appropriation as a feminist heroine and inspiration to modern artists six centuries after her death. Not all of the artistic attention Christine has garnered has been positive, however, and we will see that some of the censure she has endured takes the form of surprisingly modern cultural endeavours.

But first, we must return to Christine's time and to the city which fostered her creative activity and whose flourishing literary and artistic culture allowed it to thrive. Let us begin with a journey into fourteenth-century Paris.

Charles v reading in the Louvre library, miniature from a 1372 French translation of John of Salisbury's 12th-century *Polycraticus*.

ONE

A Visit to Christine de Pizan's Paris

I journeyed for many days until the light of the country I was approaching appeared to me from afar . . . Discerning her glory better the nearer I approached, I finished my long journey in her principal city, which was called the second Athens.
Le Livre de l'avision Cristine[1]

I n 1368, when Christine de Pizan, who was then around four years old, arrived in Paris from Venice, the French royal court that received her was itself undergoing renewal. At thirty years old and having only succeeded to the throne four years earlier, Charles v was a young king. His wife, Johanna of Bourbon, was expecting her first child, the future Charles vi. As for Paris, the city was a thriving cultural centre and thanks to her father's position as court astrologer, Christine was installed in its heart from the moment she set foot in the city. It was in Paris and at court that she would spend the next fifty years of her life. As a courtier, Christine was afforded a privileged insight into the various cultural and political phenomena of the time. While her situation made the practicalities of becoming a writer more accessible, the political climate provided plentiful material for her writings.

Given that so much of the late medieval period in France was otherwise characterized by turmoil, it was fortunate that Christine's childhood and early adulthood were relatively free from disturbance. In her works, Christine would look back on this peaceful period with great nostalgia, entreating her politically active readers to bring about a return to the peace and good fortune that she and France had enjoyed when she was a girl. The decades immediately preceding the family's arrival in Paris had told a very different story. These years had been marked by the outbreak of the Hundred Years War in 1337, the arrival of the plague in 1348, which had killed around a third of the population of Paris, and civil unrest. By 1368 these troubles were not far from the forefront of collective memory, but the city was now enjoying a period of relative calm and prosperity. The civil uprisings had largely been quashed and the plague had dissipated from the capital by 1350. Following an unsuccessful attempt by the English to take the city in 1360, the Hundred Years War was in the midst of a truce that lasted until 1369. Paris itself was – for now at least – safe from the immediate threat of war.

Charles v's reign was particularly peaceful compared to those of his father and of his son. Rather than conflict, his was marked by the undertaking of great cultural and architectural projects that earned him the nickname 'The Wise'. The ongoing conflict with the English was never far from Charles's mind, though, and his cultural endeavours were part of a wider defensive and political strategy.

Paris and Its Medieval Populace

Taking a step back from important political events for now, let us explore the city of Paris itself. What was it like when Christine de Pizan lived there? In 1380 the area inside the city walls was approximately a tenth of the size of today's metropolis; it was inhabited by some 130–150,000 people – between 10.5 and 12 per cent of the population of Paris in 2020. That number had

recently swelled, since hundreds of people dwelling outside the
city had moved into its safer confines with the onset of the
Hundred Years War.[2] By 1400 the population had grown to
200,000, making Paris the largest city in the Western world.
The spires of its devotional buildings stood tall on the city's
landscape, but its architecture was otherwise less vertically ambitious than the multi-storied Haussmannian residences that have
typified Parisian streets since the nineteenth century. The city
could not therefore accommodate as many people per square
kilometre as it can today: whereas the current population den-
sity of Paris is roughly five hundred people per hectare (two
hundred per acre), in 1400 it would have been closer to 360.

Like modern Paris, the medieval city varied enormously in
terms of its population, particularly in the disparity between
the very rich and the very poor. At the end of the thirteenth
century 70 per cent of the population was too poor to be taxed,
but 1 per cent of the richest citizens paid 80 per cent of all
dues collected.[3] The wealthy had no shortage of places in which
to spend their money. The area just north of the Tour Saint-
Jacques on the Right Bank (the Rue Saint-Martin, Rue de la
Verrerie and Rue des Lombards in the modern fourth arrondissement) was known for its luxury markets, selling wares of ivory,
bronze, gold and silver in addition to fine drapery and garments.[4]
Books were another luxury. The king coveted illuminated manuscripts and the words of ancient philosophers, and members of
the Parisian nobility were encouraged to follow his example in
order to maintain their rank. Such works were treated like jewels
or other precious items, often exchanged as gifts at court on
New Year's Day.

Since its foundation in the early thirteenth century, the
University of Paris had remained a leading centre for theolog-
ical and philosophical thinking. Medieval Paris was home to
more clerics than any other city in Europe (clerics being

scholars who may have taken some kind of minor religious orders). Approximately 10 per cent of the medieval population were members of the clergy or students, many of whom lived in the colleges that were dotted around the Left Bank. The fact that these clerics were male meant that Paris was home to more men than women. A consequence of this was the development of trades that could tend to male needs – including prostitution, which itself was not condemned in Paris. Although the Church frowned on it, it was perceived as a necessary evil. Much like purging one's bowels, sexual desire was seen as an unsavoury physical need that had to be provided for and regulated. And so, just as in 1370 when the first sewer had been built to deal with the population's physical waste, brothels had been established.[5]

Although this is one aspect of the city from which she was somewhat removed, Christine herself was not unaware of this less respectable side of Parisian life. A chapter of her book *Le Livre des trois vertus* (The Book of the Three Virtues), an instruction manual intended primarily for noble and bourgeois women, discusses prostitutes in a chapter entitled 'Women Who Lead Immoral Lives'. Here, she condemns these women for what she perceives as a choice on their part to lead a dishonourable and abominable life, somewhat callously stereotyping them as drunken brawlers. Christine believes prostitutes have three excuses – all equally invalid – for being unwilling to abandon their way of life:

> One is that the dishonest men who frequent them would not permit it; the second reason is that the world who thinks them abominable would reject them and chase them away . . . the third reason is that they would not know what to live on, for they have no profession.[6]

Christine goes on to suggest alternative professions that repentant prostitutes might turn to, such as becoming laundresses, spinners or nurses. She says: 'if she has a body strong enough to do evil things and to suffer bad nights, beatings and other misfortunes, she would be strong enough to earn a living.'[7] While her belief in the charity of others to take in and employ repentant prostitutes is admirable, some might accuse Christine of being rather unworldly here. No matter how penitent individual prostitutes might be, whether potential employers would have viewed them with much sympathy is debatable. But Christine's attitude might be excused by the fact that she was probably not aiming to counsel prostitutes themselves (as she herself points out, they were unlikely to read or even be able to access her book), and so her advice is addressed to upper-class readers whom she aimed to persuade to act charitably towards them.

Christine's chapter on prostitutes is also notable for being written *by* a woman rather than simply *about* them. Although discourse about prostitutes in the Middle Ages was not lacking, this was a subject typically only broached by men. As she reminds readers in her writings, Christine had also experienced at first hand how much a paid occupation and sympathetic employer could turn around a woman's personal misfortunes. Her own example illustrated the benefits that might come from women extending their generosity towards the less fortunate and made a point about the importance of charitable behaviour in general. Christine's experience could also inspire other women to support themselves, though she shows this could not be done without difficulty and perseverance.

Geography and Architecture

Let us give the modern visitor a sense of the geography of medieval Paris. At the turn of the fifteenth century, the area known as the Tuileries, now the site of the Tuileries Gardens, stood at the western extremity of the city just outside the newly built perimeter walls, while the Bastille fortress (which famously fell during the 1789 Revolution) had just been constructed on its eastern boundary. What are now the bustling streets of Montmartre were cultivated fields, lying some 2 kilometres (1¼ mi.) beyond the north of the city walls. To the south, meanwhile, the city was largely dominated by religious communities and the university, which occupies the same site on the Left Bank of the river Seine to this day. Beyond this, there was little to be found except farmland.

Although the boundaries and size of the city are different to those of today's Paris, for a late medieval visitor, many of the city's most important landmarks would have been the same as they are for our modern tourist. Chief among those are its two most prominent devotional buildings, the Gothic cathedral of Notre-Dame, whose construction began in 1160, and the Sainte-Chapelle, which was built between 1243 and 1248. The latter building originally formed part of the Palais de la Cité – the seat of royal power in Paris since the Roman era, of which much still remains. Although now thought of primarily as a museum, the stronghold of the Louvre was another significant fortress in the landscape of medieval Paris. Despite these survivors, many medieval landmarks have long since vanished, but their presence is sometimes evoked in the names of streets and districts. Châtelet, whose name literally means 'small castle', is a prime example. The memory of the stronghold that stood at the Place du Châtelet for almost a thousand years survives only in the name of a busy metro station and of a few surrounding streets. Elsewhere, the Rue des Lavandières (Washerwomen Street), Rue du Fauconnier (Falconer Street) or Rue de la Parcheminerie (Parchment Street) conjure up the kinds of activities that once took place in these ancient thoroughfares.

Scene depicting October, with the Louvre fortress in the background, miniature created by the Limbourg brothers for *Les Très Riches Heures du duc de Berry*, 1411–16.

In the Middle Ages, fine aristocratic mansions known as *hôtels* proliferated in the Marais district and in the area to the north of the Louvre. These residences generally consisted of several buildings enclosing a central courtyard. The royal princes each owned several *hôtels* – Charles v's brother, the Duke of Berry, had more than ten inside the city walls alone, as well as several castles outside the capital. Only a few medieval Parisian *hôtels* remain, although a rare survivor, just around the corner from where Charles v's main residence once stood in the Marais, is the fourteenth-century Hôtel de Sens, part of which now houses a library. Nearby, on the Rue des Archives, the Hôtel de Soubise also dates to the fourteenth century, although it underwent extensive remodelling in the seventeenth. Medieval examples might be scarce, but these long-lost buildings are again evoked through place names, such as the Rue des Tournelles, also in the Marais, which marks the location of the fourteenth-century

Tour Jean-sans-Peur stands out in a row of Haussmann buildings on Rue Étienne Marcel in Paris.

Hôtel des Tournelles – an *hôtel* that was owned by Charles v's son Louis of Orleans.

On the whole, the fate of non-aristocratic Parisian buildings has been similar to those constructed for its wealthier ancestors, although those that do remain offer us an insight into the more ordinary side of life in medieval Paris. The oldest house in the city, built by the bookseller Nicolas Flamel in 1407, stands at present-day 51 Rue de Montmorency in the third arrondissement. It still bears a (restored) Gothic inscription above its door along with the carved initials of its first owner and some decorative figures of angels, although a fresco depicting Nicolas and his wife Pernelle has sadly vanished. Appropriately, the stones of this three-storey building are the colour of aged parchment. Now a restaurant, its ground floor was once occupied by two shops that were accessed through the wooden doors that remain on the left and right of the building's facade. The middle door provided access to a spiral staircase through which day-labourers gained their lodgings on the upper floors. Nicolas Flamel's house offers a rare glimpse into what a secular medieval dwelling would have been like. Closer to the river, two tall timber-framed gabled medieval buildings on the Rue François Miron still stretch up to heights of five and six storeys. Around the corner, where the quiet, cobbled alleyway of the Rue des Barres meets the Rue du Grenier-sur-l'Eau, the beamed facade and carved stone turret of another fifteenth-century structure transport any onlooker back to the medieval city.

Part of an exceptional building of Christine's era that remains is the Tour Jean-sans-Peur in the second arrondissement. Standing some six storeys in height, this tower was once part of a much larger *hôtel*. It is named after its owner, John of Burgundy, who was known as 'The Fearless'. He was Charles v's nephew and sometime regent for Charles vi. His tower is now a museum dedicated to the Middle Ages that lies off the beaten track and

welcomes fewer tourists than it deserves to. The tower itself was built by John between 1409 and 1411 as part of an extensive remodelling of the *hôtel* on the site. As a testament to its former size, the highest point of its roof only just fails to measure up to that of its next-door neighbour, an eight-storey Haussmann apartment block. Just below its eaves, the top floor contains a chamber, believed to be the one in which John himself received visitors. It might be no more than clever room-dressing on the part of the museum's curators, but the chamber bears a remarkable resemblance to the room in which John is depicted in a manuscript that he owned. If this was in fact John's chamber, then this is one of the only still-extant medieval rooms in modern-day Paris that Christine is likely to have set foot in. We know that Christine visited John in another of the royal palaces – she tells us of her being summoned to meet him at the Louvre at the start of *Le Livre des fais et bonnes meurs du sage roy Charles v* (The Book of the Deeds and Good Conduct of the Wise King Charles v), so it is not impossible that she also visited him here – perhaps to deliver one of the many manuscripts that she offered him.

Without a doubt, one of the most impressive buildings in Christine's time was the new royal residence of the Hôtel Saint-Pol, whose construction was begun by Charles v in 1361. Almost no trace survives of the magnificent collection of buildings that formed this noble residence – one of many such dwellings that were once abundant in the Marais part of town. Only a fragment of its architecture remains: a wall that formed part of its church, now situated at the junction of modern-day Rue Saint-Paul and Rue Neuve-Saint-Pierre. As well as an array of buildings, the Hôtel Saint-Pol comprised extensive gardens, an aviary and even a menagerie – the memory of which is conserved in the name of the road, Rue des Lions Saint-Paul, which today crosses the *hôtel*'s

'John the Fearless in Counsel', miniature from Pierre Salmon, *Réponses à Charles vi et Lamentation au roi sur son état, c.* 1410.

Paris in the early fifteenth century

1. Le Louvre
2. Porte Saint Honoré
3. Hôtel d'Orléans
4. Les Halles
5. Saints-Innocents
6. Châtelet
7. Saint-Jacques
8. Hôtel de Sens
9. Hôtel Saint-Pol
10. Hôtel des Tournelles
11. Bastide Saint-Antoine
12. Palais de la Cité
    and Sainte Chapelle
13. Notre-Dame
14. Tournelle fortress
15. Hôtel de Cluny
16. La Sorbonne
17. Sainte Geneviève
18. Porte Saint Jacques
19. Hôtel de Soubise
20. Nicolas Flamel's House
21. Hôtel de Bourgogne (Tour
    Jean-Sans-Peur)
22. Tour Barbeau

I.   Rue Saint-Martin
II. Rue Saint-Antoine
III. Rue de la Parcheminerie
IV. Rue Saint-Jacques
V.   Rue Neuve-Notre-Dame

Built-up areas
Colleges and University
buildings
Other significant buildings

Tuileries

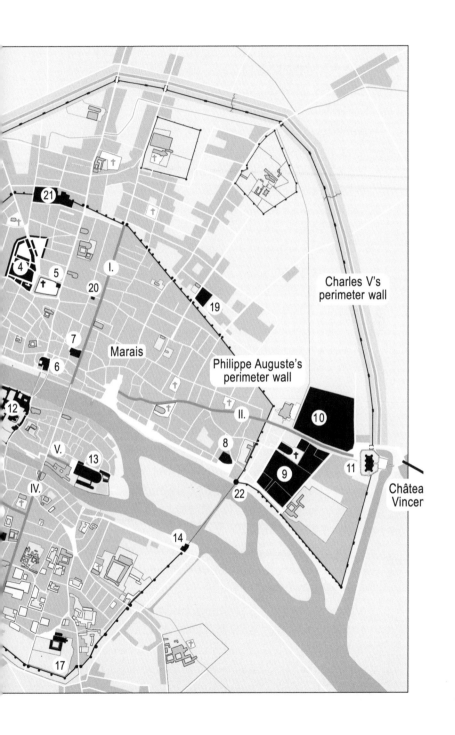

Charles V's
perimeter wall

Philippe Auguste's
perimeter wall

Marais

Châtea
Vincer

former site. Although the king had several other properties in
Paris, Saint-Pol was his main residence. It was here that he enter-
tained notable guests including, in 1378, Emperor Charles IV of
Luxembourg – as Christine recounts in some detail in her biography of Charles V, the *Fais et bonnes meurs*. In fact, it is largely
down to Christine's efforts in commemorating her family's protector that so much is known about the king's endeavours and
his building enterprises in Paris. She expresses her admiration
for his architectural ambition at several points in the text:

> Our King Charles was a wise artist and showed himself to
> be a true architect of determined vision and a cautious
> planner. This can be seen in the fine foundations he had
> built in several locations, constructing fine and noble
> edifices, churches as well as castles and other buildings,
> in Paris and abroad.[8]

Christine goes on to list the devotional buildings that Charles
V founded, restored or extended, the castles that he renovated,
his building of a new bridge across the river Seine, and the new
city walls whose construction he had taken over from his father.

These architectural projects reflect the fact that, in the
middle of the fourteenth century, the threat of war remained a
serious concern. In 1370 the English set fire to a number of villages on the outskirts of Paris. The king would have been able
to see these fires in the distance even as he observed the building works taking place in the city – many of which were being
constructed precisely in order to defend against any English
advances. The most notable such structure to be built was a new
perimeter boundary wall, whose construction had been started
by King John II in 1358, a portion of which can still be seen on
a visit to the Louvre's subterranean foundations. The new wall,
the fourth defensive barricade to be built around Paris, replaced

the twelfth-century enclosure constructed by King Philippe Auguste. Unlike previous walls, which had surrounded the city in its entirety, this one encompassed only the Right Bank, the direction from which the danger of an English offensive was most pressing. Many buildings located outside this perimeter were destroyed, forcing their occupants to move into a safer place inside the walls. At 4.9 kilometres (3 mi.), the new wall was twice the length of the equivalent section of the previous fortification and, unlike the old wall, it was designed to be able to withstand the impact of field artillery. Another sign of the architects' concern with military threat: the new rampart on the Right Bank comprised a mere six gates, whereas the previous wall had featured almost double the number of apertures although it was only half the length of the new section.[9]

The perpetual English threat affected the situation of the royal family, too. Part of what rendered the Saint-Pol residence so attractive was that it offered a good level of protection from any potential attack. It had been built so that it backed onto the newly constructed fortress of the Bastide Saint-Antoine – later known as the Bastille – on the eastern extremity of the new city wall.[10] From Saint-Pol, the king could safely and easily travel to his other residences: a safe journey to the Château de Vincennes was ensured by accessing the gate adjacent to the Bastille, and the Louvre and Palais de la Cité could both be reached by river from within the confines of the *hôtel* walls.

What about Christine and her family? On the modern-day Quai des Célestins on the bank of the river Seine, a short stroll from where the Saint-Pol residence once stood, a modest plaque informs passers-by that this was once the location of the Tour Barbeau, formerly part of Philippe Auguste's city walls. Few will have heard of this former landmark, yet this is where Christine and her family are believed to have lived from 1380, when Charles v made a gift of the tower to her husband, Etienne de Castel.[11] Although nothing remains of Christine's former residence, it must have been quite an enviable position. The Tour Barbeau complex was perched on the bank of the river, its buildings, gardens and inhabitants enclosed within a protective stone wall. In some of the illustrations seen in her works, Christine is represented at study or writing in a chamber whose shape suggests it forms part of a tower. It is often assumed that the tower must be the one that housed the royal library in the Louvre palace, but it is tantalizing to think that representations such as these might in fact show the author at work in her own home.

Miniature of Christine at study, from *Le Livre du chemin de long estude*, 1403–4.

Charles v, the Wise King

As the title of the work suggests, a large proportion of Christine's
biography of Charles v, the *Fais et bonnes meurs*, is given over to
describing the king's good deeds and achievements. Throughout
the text, Christine often simultaneously focuses on two types of
achievements: his architectural undertakings and his learning
and great wisdom. The language that she uses can sometimes
pertain to either undertaking, as if describing one inevitably
entails the other:

> He loved fine books on the topics of moral sciences,
> describing noteworthy stories on Roman governance,
> or other such praiseworthy teachings, and delighted in
> listening to them. He enjoyed any work that was skilfully
> crafted, refined and polished – rich ornaments or fine
> edifices – and had many forged across his lands, in Paris
> as well as elsewhere.[12]

Nowhere is the combination of Charles v's architectural
vision and love of learning rendered more clearly than in one
of his most ambitious undertakings, the construction of a new
royal library. This project involved not only creating a brand-
new physical, architectural library space, but commissioning new
literary material for it to contain. For these two purposes,
Charles v invested in a private specialist workforce that included
an architect – Raymond du Temple – various writers and scribes
who would pen multiple copies of 34 new works that he commissioned for the library, and the first royal librarian, a man named
Giles Malet.

Over a period of some twenty years, while the books that
would go on to grace the king's collection were being prepared, the
royal library was relocated from the single storey it had occupied

in a tower of the Palais de la Cité since the end of the thirteenth century to a new home in the Louvre. The library that Charles v commissioned was, to all intents and purposes, a 'physical monument to learning'.[13] Relocating the library was a significant part of a wider renovation of the Louvre – an architectural redevelopment that amplified, rather than simply renovated, the palace's existing structures. Charles v's efforts to redevelop the Louvre reinscribed his dynasty within that of his ancestors – notably Philippe Auguste, the first king of all of France, who had constructed the Louvre in 1190. Philippe Auguste also provided a model for Charles v's current political challenges, as he had successfully regained certain French territories from the English. Mirroring the achievements of his ancestors gave the impression of a legitimate, stable and powerful monarch. The works commissioned for the library served a similar legitimizing strategy. Many of them stressed the descendance of Charles's royal line from Trojan origins, for instance – a requirement for any legitimate French monarch.[14] The expansive new library occupied three floors of the *tour de la fauconnerie* (falconry tower), which was now renamed the *tour de la librairie* (library tower); it was accessible only via the king's private chambers – an architectural reminder of the king's direct association with learning. Once in its new home, the king's book collection continued to expand: the inventories carried out in 1373 and 1380 show an increase of some 40 per cent in the number of manuscripts on the first floor of the library, which housed texts relating to history, law and governance.[15] Extending the royal library was a work-in-progress to which the king and his craftsmen devoted their lives.

For Charles v as for Christine, architectural works were inextricable from learning and wisdom – and by extension, royal power: 'with the Louvre library looming over the Paris landscape as an extension of the king's private chambers, library visitors would have had visual evidence on a grand scale of the powerful

role knowledge was afforded in the kingdom.'[16] Estimates of
just how extensive the king's book collection would have been
vary, but most calculations put it between 1,000 and 1,300
manuscripts. By modern standards, this may not seem like an
especially large collection. However, for comparison, the sizeable
library of the University of Paris was only fractionally larger –
estimated at around 1,500 volumes in the same period. In 1369,
over a century before the Vatican Library was founded, the pon-
tifical library in Rome held 2,059 volumes. A few decades later
in England, what is now the Bodleian Library at the University
of Oxford was essentially formed by a single donation of 281
manuscripts by Humphrey, Duke of Gloucester. So large was this
donation that a new building had to be constructed to house it.[17]
By comparison, in 1397 the library of Humphrey's great-uncle
Thomas of Woodstock had numbered a mere 84 volumes.[18] The
same trend in the acquisition of books and expansion of libraries can be seen in the inventories of the Burgundian library in
Paris, which comprised seventy volumes on the death of Philip
of Burgundy in 1404, 248 on the death of his successor in 1419,
and by the time of the death of the next Duke of Burgundy in
1467 had reached 876 tomes – more than a tenfold increase in
under seventy years.[19]

Although these numbers might seem small to us, the size of
medieval manuscripts means that the books would have taken
up a much larger amount of space than the same number of
volumes would do today. Luxurious manuscripts, which were
often those containing texts dedicated to particular patrons,
could be considerable in size. An extreme example is the work
known as the Vernon Manuscript, prepared towards the end of
the fourteenth century and the largest surviving manuscript
written in Middle English. This hefty volume measures some
54 × 39 centimetres (21¼ × 15¼ in.) and weighs 22 kilograms
(48½ lb) – almost unfathomably heavy for a book.[20] Naturally,

not all medieval books were this large, but even small tomes or manuscripts could be quite sturdy, especially once they had been finished with wooden plates and wrapped in a leather binding. The manuscripts Christine prepared demonstrate the diversity of sizes that medieval books could take. Her largest volume is the manuscript now known as Paris, Bibliothèque Nationale de France, MS fr. 603, which measures 37 × 27 centimetres (14½ × 10½ in.) and contains two of her works. Libraries do not tend to list the thickness of the books in their safekeeping, but a sense of its width can be gained from observing the number of sheets of parchment it contains, which in this case is 242 folios. Parchment is considerably thicker than modern paper – a single sheet can be as thick as around seven sheets of standard copier paper. A volume of 242 sheets of parchment could therefore be as thick as one containing up to seven times that amount of paper. At the other end of the scale, Christine's smallest manuscript, a slender tome of 97 folios whose modern shelf-mark is Paris, Bibliothèque Nationale de France, MS fr. 24786, measures just 17 × 12 centimetres (6¾ × 4¾ in.) – similar in dimensions to a modern paperback. These are, however, outliers in Christine's manuscript production; the typical size of the volumes she presented to noble patrons is around 28 × 19 centimetres (11 × 7½ in.) – a fraction smaller than standard A4 size or modern printer paper. These manuscripts are around 7 centimetres (2¾ in.) thick.

Whatever their finished size, medieval books were very expensive. So much so that, until the arrival of printing in the middle of the fifteenth century, the written word was almost exclusively the preserve of the nobility or the very wealthy. As many manuscripts were made on commission, as opposed to ready-made items bought off the shelf, each aspect of the craftsmanship was usually paid for separately (as opposed to a book being purchased in a single transaction). It is therefore hard to estimate the total cost of an entire volume. Nevertheless, surviving records give us some indication of the scale of the expense involved. For instance, in the second half of the fourteenth century, the cost of illuminating the large initials of an English manuscript now known as the Lytlington Missal was £22 – representing more than the annual income of the entire estate that paid for the work.[21] In Paris, Louis of Orleans' records indicate that he paid up to 400 francs for a sumptuous French Bible. There is no straightforward system for converting medieval money into modern equivalents, but to put this into perspective, a good horse at the time could be purchased for around 30 francs.[22] Louis could therefore have bought more than thirteen horses for the same price as his illuminated Bible. There will be more to say later on the practical and collaborative nature of the book and manuscript trades, but for now, I simply remark that a vast number of artisans would have been involved in making any single book. With its abundance of clerical staff and artisans who could see to the production and technical aspects of bookmaking as well as its luxury markets in which the requisite materials could be obtained, Paris was an ideal city for such an enterprise.

Because of the scale of the expansion of his personal library, instead of paying a series of artisans piecemeal for individual pieces of work, Charles v took a different approach. Many of the artisans, illuminators and writers who were commissioned on his behalf worked exclusively for the royal court. This phenomenon was not entirely new: Charles v's mother, Joan of Burgundy, and his grandmother Blanche of Navarre had both also invested heavily in book culture, while his father, John ii, had provided several illuminators with a fixed salary for their services as royal painters.[23] Nevertheless, the scale of the changes brought by Charles v to the royal collections was unprecedented. Although for Charles v architecture and wisdom often went together, the fact that the annual pension provided to the writers

Nicole Oresme and Raoul de Presles was four times the income given to his architect is revealing of how much he valued their intellectual work.[24] It is perhaps difficult for us to appreciate just how astonishing the finished product, which combined architectural magnificence with finely decorated and carefully crafted manuscripts, must have been. Deborah McGrady imagines a striking scene:

> When entering the first floor of the Louvre library, visitors would certainly have been dazzled by the multicoloured silk wrappings and the many silver manuscript clasps that glittered from panelled library recesses. Perhaps some of the king's books were left open on the new shelving so that viewers could catch a glimpse of the even greater riches contained within.[25]

That the library itself could only be gained via the king's private chambers – and was therefore only accessible on the king's invitation and to a very select few – would only have increased its splendour.

Charles VI and the End of Peace

Given the profound impact that Charles V had on French, and especially Parisian, culture, it is hard to believe he reigned for only sixteen years. When he died at the age of 42 in 1380, he left behind a significant cultural legacy and, although the final years of his reign were not entirely peaceful, they were marked by a feeling that good fortune had at long last returned to France. Between 1369 and 1375 the gains that the English had made against the French had gradually been reversed. France, and its capital city in particular, was flourishing. With the succession of Charles VI, this period of peace and prosperity slowly came to an end. At eleven years old, the new king was too young to reign, and so until he reached his majority eight years later, France was ruled by a regent – Charles V's brother and the new king's uncle, Philip of Burgundy.

Charles VI had not long been able to rule independently when, in 1392, he experienced his first public bout of mental illness – often referred to as madness, but probably a form of schizophrenia or psychosis. The following year, an event took place that was to profoundly change the fates of Charles VI and of France. It was a masked ball at the Hôtel Saint-Pol, for which the king and four others had decided to dress up as 'wild men'. The group arrived at the party dressed in costumes made of linen that had been soaked in resin and covered in hemp and dried leaves. As they leapt about in a frenzied dance, a guest approached with a flaming torch, intent on revealing their identities. He leaned in a little too close such that sparks from his torch alighted onto the highly flammable costumes, all of which were immediately set aflame. Of the five dancers, all perished except the king. Charles was saved only because his sister-in-law, the Duchess of Berry, put out the fire by wrapping her skirts around him. This might have just been an unfortunate accident, but in the aftermath of what became known as the 'Bal des Ardents' (Ball of the Burning Men) it was clear that Charles was not fit to rule the country and that a regent would need to govern in his place.

Unfortunately, there were several candidates for this role. Since Philip of Burgundy had already acted as regent during Charles's minority, when this new opportunity came about, he immediately seized that power for himself. By rights, however, the role should have fallen to the king's younger brother, Louis of Orleans. The subsequent disagreement between the king's uncle and brother set in motion a feud that would tear apart the royal family for decades, leading to a nation divided by a civil war known as the Armagnac–Burgundian conflict. The

The 'Bal des Ardents' in which four men lost their lives, but
Charles VI survived. Miniature from Jean Froissart, *Chroniques*
(the 'Harley Froissart'), c. 1470–72.

main opponents in this war would be John of Burgundy and
later his own son Philip on the Burgundian side, and Louis of
Orleans on that of the Orleanists, whose cause was later taken
up by the Armagnacs. The conflict between John and Louis
simmered away for a number of years during which threats and
mediations were made on both sides, though there were also periods of truce between the parties. Their antipathy turned violent
in 1407, resulting in a period of terror that culminated in one
of the bloodiest chapters in the history of medieval Paris. The
events of the Armagnac–Burgundian conflict are complex, but
a full understanding is not necessary to appreciate the impact
of the feud on cultural production.[26]

Christine, who moved among the main players in these
conflicts, was far from eschewing the difficulties they presented.

In fact, references to the political context can be perceived in almost all of her texts, sometimes overtly, sometimes more cautiously. In *Le Livre de l'avision Cristine* (The Book of Christine's Vision) the persona of Libera (an allegorical personification of France) movingly describes the impact of civil war on France as a 'plague, which is worse than an epidemic throughout my land'.[27] Christine does more than just lament the current situation, though, and in several of her works she takes an instructive approach, actively encouraging her readers to remedy the situation. One of the texts in which she most overtly tackles the matter of civil war is the *Lamentacions sur les maux de la France* (Lamentation on France's Ills), an open letter dated 23 August 1410. This text was penned shortly after the king's uncle, John of Berry, had declined an invitation to come to Paris for political talks. In writing it, Christine partly urges John to come to Paris as planned, and partly bolsters the role of the queen, Isabeau of Bavaria, as mediator in the crisis.[28] In a moving section of the letter, which opens with a description of the author struggling to curb the flow of tears that hamper her writing, Christine attempts to rouse the queen to action:

> Oh, crowned Queen of France, are you still sleeping? Who prevents you from restraining now this side of your kin and putting an end to this deadly enterprise? Do you not see the heritage of your noble children at stake? You, the mother of the noble heirs of France, Revered Princess, who but you can do anything, and who will disobey your sovereignty and authority, if you rightly want to mediate a peace?[29]

Other contemporary writers also attempted to intervene in the crisis. In his *Quadrilogue invectif* of 1422, Alain Chartier showed a personified representation of France in a state of disarray: her hair is dishevelled, her robes are torn, her castle

is falling down. Chartier incited all members of society to take
responsibility for the state of the country. Although, like
Chartier, Christine makes use of allegory to discuss political
matters elsewhere, she uses no such literary artifice in her letter.
Unlike her contemporaries, she was not afraid of appearing in
a personal and emotional capacity to create an impact in her
political discourse.

Queen Isabeau of Bavaria, the wife of Charles VI, was a
frequent recipient of Christine's writings, including her political works. Two extensive collections of Christine's works were
presented to Isabeau some fifteen years apart (Chantilly, Musée
Condé, MS 492–3 and London, British Library, Harley MS 4431,
now known as 'The Queen's Manuscript'), as were several of
her individual texts and poems. Many of these writings engage
directly with contemporary political conflicts, frequently
imploring the queen to intervene and mediate between the
warring factions in the Civil War – a role she took up on several occasions. One reason for appealing to Isabeau was that
she too was a strong contender for the role of regent; Christine's
subtle attempts to influence political events can be witnessed
in her reminding readers of queens who had taken on such roles
in French history in *Le Livre de la cité des dames* (The Book of
the City of Ladies). As far as the Civil War was concerned,
Christine was in the rather unusual – and potentially hazardous
– position of having patrons on both sides of the conflict. In
order to ensure her safety, it was paramount for her to remain
neutral, or, at the very least, to give the appearance of being so.
Although for a long time it was believed that, because she had
worked for the Burgundian household, Christine supported the
Burgundian faction in the Civil War, she in fact never wavered
from supporting the Orleans side of the conflict.[30] It would
have been dangerous for her to outwardly champion Louis,
however, and so she instead channelled her support towards

Isabeau, who was a close ally of Louis'. This discretion allowed Christine some semblance of neutrality.

Given her Orleanist tendencies, how was Christine to respond to a commission from the leader of the Burgundian faction, Philip of Burgundy, to compose a book in honour of his brother, Charles v – a man whom she evidently admired? To accept this commission would be to go against her own political conscience and could be interpreted as showing support for the Burgundians. Yet they made for extremely dangerous enemies, so refusing was not an option. Christine had no choice but to accept. She composed the work that Philip requested in honour of the beloved king, but in doing so attributes qualities to him that are connected with the Burgundian enemy and rival, Louis of Orleans. Over many chapters of *Fais et bonnes meurs*, Christine describes the qualities and virtues associated with the king's advisors, but Philip's achievements are described only in terms of duties carried out in his own territories. Not once does Christine praise him for his work as regent.[31]

Just as Christine's disdain for the Burgundians was hidden, her support for Louis of Orleans was similarly concealed. Her Orleanist tendencies can be inferred in *Le Livre du chemin de long estude* (The Book of the Path of Long Study), where the qualities that are necessary in the man who would be 'king of the world' align with Louis. Specifically, it is said that the ideal ruler must be descended from a line of Trojans and associated with wisdom – these are qualities linked closely with Charles v, Louis' father (and by extension with Louis), but not with John. In *L'Epistre Othea* (The Epistle of Othea) the costumes and the emblems that Louis and Hector of Troy bear in the illuminations imply a correspondence between the princes, from whom the French nobility claimed ancestry.[32] Hector is praised in terms that celebrate his legitimacy and military feats:

> . . . you, Hector,
> Noble and powerful prince,
> Successor of the noble Trojans,
> The heir of Troy and its citizens,
> Ever distinguished in arms.[33]

No such praise was ever granted to Christine's Burgundian patrons, about whom she was comparatively silent. Where she does pay homage to them, it is limited to a subject that was always very close to her heart and her fondest wish: the ability to bring about peace.

Unfortunately, Christine's peaceful desires were not satisfied during her lifetime. In November 1407 John, the new Duke of Burgundy, brutally murdered his nephew Louis on the Rue Vieille du Temple. This was an act of shocking duplicity, given that only three days earlier the two dukes had made a promise of friendship in an act of ritual brotherhood where John had sworn an oath to God to put aside his enmity. Christine did not forget John's betrayal. In the decade since the Armagnac–Burgundian conflict had turned violent, the conflict with the English had resurged, and the Burgundians had effectively paved the way for the English to inflict a crushing defeat for the French at the battle of Agincourt in 1415. Composed in 1418, Christine's *Epistre de la prison de vie humaine* (Epistle of the Prison of Human Life) denounces other great treacheries from history – the poisoning of Alexander the Great and betrayal of Julius Caesar – and the parallel with Louis' murder is clear. Christine's message is evident: had John not betrayed and murdered Louis, the English would not have been able to invade so easily, and the Agincourt disaster would never have taken place. That the Burgundians had taken the side of the English in the war had only redoubled their enemy in Christine's eyes. Ultimately, it became clear that peace between the Orleans-Armagnacs and Burgundians would not be possible and, in a massacre that culminated in June 1418, many of those who supported the opposing side of the faction were brutally murdered by the Burgundians in Paris. Christine herself was in the city at this time, and in all likelihood fled to the safety of a nearby abbey when the queen escaped. She never returned.

The Ramifications of War on the Cultural Landscape

What became of Paris, and Charles v's library, in the aftermath of these conflicts? The English and French signed the Treaty of Troyes in 1420, naming Henry v of England as heir and regent to the French throne. Henry died shortly thereafter, and the Duke of Bedford was appointed as regent for the new king, Henry vi. The English continued to occupy Paris until 1436. Under Bedford's custody, the last inventory of the royal library was carried out in 1424. By 1429, however, its volumes had been dispersed and to this day only around a hundred manuscripts from Charles's library – fewer than 10 per cent of the total collection – have been identified with certainty. Bedford purchased many of the tomes himself, bringing most of them back to England. This explains the presence of several notable French manuscripts in British libraries, including the infamous 'Queen's Manuscript' that Christine prepared for Queen Isabeau. This manuscript passed from Bedford's wife to her son, Anthony Woodville, and eventually came into the possession of Edward Harley, the Duke of Oxford, from whose collection it was purchased by the British Museum in 1753.[34] It is now one of the treasures of the British Library.

The Armagnac–Burgundian conflict and Hundred Years War had an enormous impact on artistic production in Paris. Although during his regency, the Duke of Bedford allowed illuminators to continue to work in Paris (he even commissioned several of the most significant illuminated manuscripts of the period to be made there), many artists left the city, relocating primarily to Rouen, Flanders or Dijon – other thriving centres of artistic and literary production. At the time, the effects of conflict on the artistic scene in Paris were devastating; it took until the second half of the fifteenth century for the cultural capital of France to recover from the ravages caused by civil and international war. Nonetheless, while Christine lived in the city, it had been thriving.

Now that we are oriented inside Christine's political and cultural landscape, we can take a closer look at contemporary Parisian book production, and her own work within it.

TWO

Christine's Artistic Vision

One cannot find an artisan to equal her in the whole city of
Paris, where the best in the world are found.
Le Livre de la cité des dames[1]

O
f the many trades that were thriving in late medieval
Paris, bookmaking employed one of the highest numbers of skilled artisans, each of whom carried out
particular tasks that went towards the creation of a physical
book. The sheer number of people involved in this work meant
that it was a collaborative activity that could only easily take
place within large cities, of which Paris was the most active
bookmaking centre in Europe. In addition to the technical know-
how of craftspeople and those who produced the raw materials
to make volumes, bookmaking also required the creative input
of numerous artists. The precise time at which Christine was
producing her works, the first two decades of the fifteenth
century, are regarded as a golden age of the French painted
manuscript. Christine herself was highly engaged with the network of artists and artisans who worked on every aspect of
designing and creating her manuscripts, taking full advantage
of the artisanal workforce available to her when she lived in the
city and of the ideal conditions Paris presented for an enterprising
writer.

Bookmaking and the Book Trade in Medieval Paris

The course of the Middle Ages saw the book trade expand rapidly. As it did, the number of copyists, binders, illuminators and book traders multiplied across Paris. First, they clustered around the university; they then gradually expanded across the whole of the Right Bank, eventually overflowing those boundaries and settling into the area around Notre-Dame. With the exception of parchment-making, all aspects of bookmaking took place inside medieval Paris. Parchment had to be produced outside the city partly on account of its smell (which involved, among other things, large quantities of lime) but also for practical purposes, since parchment-making relied on a steady supply of animal skins, which came from the abattoirs that were themselves located in the country. Once the animal skins had been treated, stretched, scraped, dried and cut to size, they were brought to the city to be traded by its many 'parchmenters', or parchment-traders, who soon gave their name to the Rue de la Parcheminerie in the modern-day Latin Quarter. Many parchmenters would also have acted as booksellers or *libraires*, and to this day, the area around this historic street is home to an abundance of bookshops and independent presses.

Once the raw writing material had been sourced, the city's large workforce of artisans could get to work on the complex task of creating a book. The first order was for the text to be neatly copied onto parchment of the requisite size. Since the thirteenth century, scribes and copyists had populated scriptoriums and workshops south of the river. Many of them worked out of or were based in monasteries or the educational institutions, such as the University of Paris, that dominated this part of town. Writing itself was a lengthy and uncomfortable process, which forced the individual to sit upright with both arms upheld, a pen in one hand and a knife used for sharpening the quill and erasing any mistakes in the other. The pen had to be lifted from the manuscript surface after each stroke, so scribes carefully and painstakingly copied letters onto parchment one single stroke at a time.

With the text prepared, the pages could be sent to illuminators who would adorn them with marginal decorations such as filigree motifs or vine leaves, decorated initials and – in the case of the finest manuscripts – resplendent images made using elements of gold leaf and paints derived from plants and minerals, including precious materials such as lapis lazuli. The process of making colours alone was a time-consuming exercise that had to be done in each workshop. Some colours, such as the greenish pigment verdigris, took up to six months to produce. Apprentices would first have to remove impurities from the stones required – an exercise that could last several days – or crush and boil plants before mixing them to create a pigment. The other ingredients required depended on the colour being prepared. They could include vinegar, soap, honey or lime, but also much less palatable materials such as urine, dung and even earwax.[2] Once mixed, the resulting product would be dried and ground to particles of the right size, before, finally, the crushed granules were combined with grindings of gum mixed with water or glair (a preparation made from egg white) to form a paint. The resulting product would then be quickly tested for transparency before, in most cases, needing to be used immediately. The fact that colours were quick to spoil is one of the reasons why they had to be made in-house rather than purchased elsewhere: they simply did not have a long enough shelf-life to be sold in a shop. All of these processes varied enormously from pigment to pigment, requiring a good amount of expertise on the apprentice's part.

This begins to illustrate just how much labour went into creating a single illumination – and how costly it was. Because of these high costs, funds sometimes ran out before manuscripts were finished, with the final stages most often those that were left incomplete. Once the text and illuminations were in place, the individual folded sheets (which collectively formed 'quires') would normally be stitched together and bound in silk or leather for a specific patron. However, if funds suddenly ran dry or the market unexpectedly changed, sheets sometimes remained unbound and the spaces left for illuminations unfilled – mere placeholders for miniatures there was no longer time or money to realize. This was the fate of some copies of Christine's works: a copy of *Le Livre du chemin de long estude* (The Book of the Path of Long Study) has blank spaces left for five miniatures and a compilation of her various works, which was copied from one of her luxury presentation manuscripts, has spaces for six.[3] At this point in the Middle Ages, most books were prepared on demand, either upon a patron's request or as a gift on the author's part (often in anticipation of some kind of reward). But because illuminated manuscripts took so long to prepare, it was not uncommon for the person who had commissioned the work to die before it had been completed. Sometimes a new patron (often the original patron's heir) might continue to fund the work so that it could be completed, but often it simply stopped at whatever stage it had reached.

With the exception of parchmenters, it was untenable to live off a single one of the various trades involved in bookmaking, so individuals tended to exercise several functions. An artisan who might specialize in bookbinding, for instance, would also act as a copyist on occasion, or be able to carry out certain elements of decoration. For this reason, different artisans often collaborated. Some individuals worked within the same workshop; others worked with members of neighbouring ateliers. As such, it made sense for the workshops of book artisans to be located in the same areas of the city as the scriptoriums, or 'scribal workshops' – they especially clustered in the area around the Rue Saint-Jacques in the Latin Quarter and later the Rue Neuve Notre-Dame. This latter street, which once directly faced Notre-Dame cathedral, has long since disappeared, although its outline is still marked in light stones in the grey cobbles on the Parvis Notre-Dame. It was once renowned for its book artisans. Workshops themselves varied in size from just one or two individuals to much larger ateliers – one illuminator-turned-book-trader named André le Musnier ran a particularly large workshop, comprising a master illuminator and several apprentices, although he relied on a scribe residing outside of Paris to copy texts for him.[4]

Although this was a thriving atmosphere for all book artisans, the book vendors and parchmenters of fourteenth-century Paris were those who did particularly well. Despite the numbers of artisans multiplying such that they began to occupy a wider geographical area, their workshops were always restricted to cheaper residences on the Left Bank, south of the river. By comparison, the demand for luxury books from non-clerical buyers became such that vendors and parchmenters moved beyond their traditional marketplace and extended onto the Right Bank, where they were especially numerous in the area around the Saints Innocents.[5] One reason why vendors fared better financially than the artisans who manufactured their products was that, as learning had gradually become more secular, there was an increasing demand for books outside of the clergy. In increasingly catering for a non-monastic audience, book traders had been able to profit from this shift, but many artisans (in particular scribes) were still clerics bound to the Church or university. Members of the traditional book trade felt threatened by this increase in competition and in 1411, in an attempt to restrict the growing book market, the king issued an ordinance forbidding anyone other than four licensed university traders from selling books. Such a mandate clearly stood no hope of being effective when the appetite for books was only growing stronger and indeed the Paris book trade only continued to expand after this date.

The secularization of the book trade could likewise not be prevented and it became an increasingly commercial enterprise. One consequence of secularization is that, whereas previously work related to the preparation of books had been undertaken by clerics (who were by nature single men), it could now be a family business. Many artisans, including André le Musnier, worked alongside their wives, but the most prolific husband-and-wife collaboration was that of Jeanne and Richard Montbaston. Though little detail has survived about how exactly the Montbastons ran their business – who was responsible for which tasks within their workshop, for instance – they are known to have run a bookmaking atelier on the Rue Neuve Notre-Dame. Fifty-three manuscripts have been attributed to the Montbaston workshop, and although it is generally assumed

Male scribe and female illuminator working side by side, believed to represent the artists Jeanne and Richard Montbaston, folio from Guillaume de Lorris and Jean de Meun, *Le Roman de la rose*, 14th century.

that the couple illuminated manuscripts together, Jeanne alone was given the accolade of 'illuminatrix libri jurata' (sworn illuminator of books), a title that was granted to only one other illuminator, a man named Pierre Dareynes in 1383. One image in the margins of a copy of *Le Roman de la rose* (The Romance of the Rose), whose decoration is attributed to the couple, depicts a man and a woman side by side working on individual sheets of parchment, the man copying text onto the page before him and the woman painting an image onto hers. Above their heads, several pages covered in writing have been hung up to dry, suggesting that the couple are working in a scriptorium. It is hard to resist the temptation to see this image as a self-portrait, showing the Montbaston couple at work in their respective functions: he as copyist, she as illuminator.

In Christine's lifetime, many of the miniaturists who produced the finest examples of illumination were working in Paris, including the artists known as the Boucicaut and Bedford Masters. Although art historians generally refer to the latter by the title of his patron, the Duke of Bedford, the Bedford Master is one of the few artisans whose real name is known: Haincelin de Haguenau. At least one miniature from Christine's illuminated manuscripts is attributed to this master – the image, which depicts a lady and a messenger exchanging a scroll, features at the start of her second *Complainte amoureuse* (Amorous Lament) in 'The Queen's Manuscript'.[6] This miniature is one of 121 illuminations in this manuscript – the most extensively decorated of Christine's volumes – the remainder of which were created by another sought-after artist known as the City of Ladies Master, an illuminator who played an important role in Christine's manuscript production and about whom more will be said later. The division of labour between illuminators in this and other manuscripts testifies to the collaborative nature of bookmaking in contemporary Paris: because artisans clustered in certain streets, when one workshop was too busy to fulfil an order, a neighbouring atelier could be called upon to take on some of the work. Since at this stage, the sheets of parchment had not yet been bound together, it was easy to distribute individual quires between workshops. From this point of view, it is actually somewhat misleading to try to attribute images to individual masters since this term suggests that they were created by an individual when they are more likely to be the work of more than one artist who operated out of the same workshop and worked in a similar style. The term 'master' also indicates a male craftsman when women are known to have carried out this work too.

Despite the abundance of skilled artisans in the city itself, for particularly important or substantial projects, artists from further afield were sometimes sought out by wealthy Parisian patrons. In such cases, the artist could be brought to the city and housed for the duration of their employment. A notable example is that of the Limbourg brothers, whom Philip of Burgundy brought to Paris so that they could work for him exclusively on an illuminated Bible. When Philip died in 1404, halfway through the brothers' four-year contract, they had together completed 384 of the Bible's images. These details give us some idea as to just how long (and how expensive – the House of Burgundy paid to house, clothe and feed the brothers for the entirety of this period) the process of creating a manuscript could be.[7]

Like all markets, the Paris book trade was enormously affected by the outbreak of war. Resources became scarce. It was increasingly difficult to get hold of the high-quality materials needed to produce fine books. Evidence of this can be seen in the paucity of the parchment in Christine's otherwise luxurious 'Queen's Manuscript'. When first studying this compilation manuscript, Sandra Hindman noticed that one of the works it contains, *L'Epistre Othea* (The Letter of Othea), had been written onto parchment much smaller in size than the pages in the rest of the volume. The individual sheets had been carefully extended by adding bands to each page – something that can be done with parchment more easily than with paper – so that the disparity in sizes would not be noticeable. Hindman concluded that this copy of the *Othea* had initially been part of a smaller volume and that its parchment was extended when it was integrated into the collected works manuscript.[8] However, when another scholar, James Laidlaw, examined the volume as part of a wide-scale enquiry into how it was made, he found that the parchment throughout the manuscript is of surprisingly poor quality.[9] For a volume whose every detail was otherwise prepared so carefully for its high-nobility beneficiary, it is astounding that superior material was not used. That better parchment was not used suggests it was probably unavailable.

'The Queen's Manuscript' was prepared between 1408 and 1414, at the height of the Civil War, and so it seems that the difficulties caused by the political climate must have been at least in part to blame, since the ongoing conflict hindered the supply of good-quality parchment coming into the city.[10] Further evidence of the adverse effect of political events on Christine's book production can be seen in her output of manuscripts. From 1401 onwards, when Paris was relatively peaceful, she had steadily increased her production of volumes, leading to an output of nine manuscripts in 1405 and again in 1406. Her production then slowed to just one book per year in 1407 and 1408, when civil troubles had begun. Although it then gradually increased again, surging to five volumes in 1410, no known manuscripts survive from the period of 1411 to 1412 or from 1415 to 1417 and only three manuscripts were produced in 1413 and 1414 together. Her most productive period therefore occurred before civil unrest reached its height. This, and the fact that Christine can be seen to have literally 'made do and mended' the material available to her in extending the pages of 'The Queen's Manuscript', shows the impact that conflict was having on Paris's creative and artistic industries.

A Glimpse into Christine's Workshop

The financial and political challenges that any enterprising author would have faced in the early fifteenth century make it all the more remarkable that Christine persevered in her manuscript production to the extent that she did. Leaving to one side the fact that she achieved all that she did as a woman, an obstacle in itself since it limited her access to the book trade, Christine's output of books in this period is exceptional on account both of its sheer volume and of her hands-on involvement in its production. Between approximately 1399 and 1420, Christine supervised the preparation of at least 54 manuscripts of her works.[11] These varied considerably in terms of their contents; many volumes contained just a single work, but several, such as 'The Queen's Manuscript', were anthologies that she presented to her patrons in magnificent compilation manuscripts.

There are few instances of medieval authors who are known to have been involved in producing their manuscripts, so how can we be so sure that this is the case for Christine? One source of evidence comes from the texts themselves, in which the author describes her involvement in writing her own material. In a chapter of *Le Livre de l'avision Cristine* (The Book of Christine's Vision), Christine describes how she went from reading ancient history, to reading poetry, until eventually she set about writing her own verses. Looking back on her literary debut in 1405, she describes how she had first composed things that were 'legieres', meaning light or basic, or made up of somewhat unsophisticated material. Christine is being a little modest here, for there is much to commend in her early works. Although her first compositions were neither as long nor as narratively complex as her later works, they nonetheless showed a level of sophistication that rivalled the poetry of her contemporaries. The humble view with which Christine regards her first works turns to pride when she recounts the progress she had made by the time she came to compose her later endeavours:

> Just like the worker who grows more clever in his work the more frequently he does it, my mind, always studying different subjects, drank in more and more new things, enriching my style with greater subtlety and more noble subjects.[12]

This same pride can be detected when she gives an account of the physical evidence of her progress: 'during this time fifteen principal volumes were compiled, excluding other individual small poems, which all together are contained in around seventy quires of large format, as can be seen.'[13] This reveals that Christine is intimately acquainted with the dimensions and physicality of her works – an indication that she was no stranger to the processes involved in preparing the volumes themselves. In this quotation, she overtly invites her reader to contemplate the artefact she has proudly laid before them – a testament to her endeavours.

Elsewhere, evidence of Christine's involvement in preparing her manuscripts can be seen from the way in which the volumes and pages are prepared. Even in the late nineteenth century, the first modern editor of Christine's works did not question that Christine had penned some of her surviving manuscripts herself, though this was not confirmed until a seminal examination of their handwriting was carried out almost a century later.[14] What these researchers found is that three different scribes (who are also known as 'hands') could be identified in her texts. These hands' writing styles are quite distinctive: one is tight and elegant, appears densely on the page and is the work of a professional scribe;[15] another is more irregular and less elegant, suggesting that it is the work of a less experienced writer.[16] But while these two hands appear only sporadically in Christine's manuscripts, a third hand permeates the volumes. It is this hand that was designated as hand X – a hand which must be Christine's.

This is unusual. No other penmanship in a medieval French literary work can be attributed with such certainty to the author. Although other authors undoubtedly also wrote out their texts themselves, it is generally not known which ones did so, or which of their manuscripts might bear their autograph writing.[17] In some texts, authors are described dictating their works to a professional scribe – a more common method of composition. Even if an author did write out their text, it is more likely that they would have penned a rough copy that would then be passed onto a scribe to be copied more neatly. In other words, although the author would compose the work, someone else would have actually written out the version that would be preserved and presented to a patron.

There are several factors that allow hand X to be identified with certainty as Christine's. In addition to its belonging to the scribe who copied the greatest number of her manuscripts, including her earliest anthologies and 'The Queen's Manuscript', that this is the author's hand can be determined by its characteristics and by what it does. In terms of its characteristics, it is the hand most like the cursive script used in chancelleries at the time. Christine's husband Etienne would have used this script in his work as a royal secretary, as would her son, meaning that this style of writing would have been familiar to Christine. She could even have learned it from Etienne – perhaps she even assisted him with his own writing on occasion. One of the rather lovely traits that distinguishes this hand from the other two is its occasional exuberant tendencies. Where space allows, it displays 'a taste for great flourishes of the pen that unfurl in a proliferation of loops and curls'.[18] On the pages of manuscripts penned by Christine, the upstrokes of the first line of letters and the downstrokes of those at the bottom of the page extend playfully into the margins. Sometimes little banderoles (ribbon-shaped scrolls) adorn the writing, curling around the extended stems of the letters. On other occasions, small doodle-like motifs have been added, delicately drawn with the tip of a quill. Flourishes of this kind are another trait typical of chancellery writing. The effect can give readers little flutters of joy as they turn the pages to see the designs appear.

As for what hand X does, in addition to being the hand responsible for copying the vast majority of Christine's manuscripts, it is also the hand that corrects the work of the other two scribes whereas, crucially, the reverse is never true.[19] Throughout copies of her work, the author's hand can be seen correcting spellings, adding missing words between the lines, inserting entries that have been omitted from the tables of contents in the margins, or sometimes even adding passages of text that had been left out. Elsewhere, traces of her preparing the layout and the general appearance of the manuscript also remain. Although many of these types of markings were intended to be erased (as most were), sometimes fragments of Christine's instructions for the insertion of details have been left in place. On folio 2v of Paris, BnF, MS fr. 848, the word 'ycy' (here), written in minute letters and very faint ink, can just be made out in the margins of the page. This is an instruction intended to tell the illuminator where to place the image. In a copy of the *Avision*, hand X has scribbled summaries of the first few chapters in the margins – these were possibly used to help her compose a preface that was added to this manuscript.[20] There were undoubtedly many more such interventions on the author's part, but most would have been erased in the final stages of manuscript preparation. Some of these vanished traces of Christine's corrections can be seen in UV light.

dieu les sacriffier de la
quel chose respondit le pro
phete / mieulx vault obe
dience que sacrefice / et
pour tant que par avivre
l'amoncion de la vray meu
se ae desober Tu seras de
boute de ton Royaume
et avont le proishete le dep
posa et en ommy David a
roy / ha chiere amie et dois
te penser que dieu dorme
ne voy te le temps que cont
ses commandemens sont
espurgnees ses iustices sur
les mauvais de droit suen
condampnez punicon maul
quilz ayent pasture pour
ficher en la quelle de la
faulse avont tout est ac
corpse / a aubon est quilz
sesensent daucune faulse
couleur de bonte faisant
leur malefice / vois tu tout
commandemit de loy mis ar
riere pour elle pasture et
nourrir sans nulle espar
gne / Que diray te de
ques fere nay pavoir que
dieu soit muable qui ne
peut estre / z s'il ne lest pon

quoy ne me touche ce
figure par semblable a
nest bope les aprestes /
bien est fol al qui mal
z bien espone / ne sont
estranges aussi apres a
voir nouvelles proyes
ilz soulorent / Et tout
comme cellui que se sent
coulpable ne vit sans le
ge de conscience / le ver
prouveur la parour de
micon ne de luy ne dep
☐ Ancore a ce propos
malefices de ceste da ma
ne parla donquee a p
Jhucrist en la parabole
la vigne sicomme il de
en l'euvangile des fau
coustieurs lesquieuls
me ilz fussent de la m
signe de ceste douleveir
par envie dauoy leve
ge nocerent il les loya
messayes iustement de
mandeur des ep fruice
comme ceste felonnie en
graft semblablement / ne
parguerent leurs glauee
droit heutier / mais com
la sentence dutine les

Erasures can be detected where the parchment has been damaged by too much rubbing (caused by scratching the ink off the surface with a knife or pumice stone) and, occasionally, blank gaps in the writing can indicate that something has been expunged.

Christine was so deeply entrenched in contemporary book-production methods that she asserted control over all aspects of how her works would appear on the written page and, by extension, exactly what her manuscripts would look like. Given her long-term collaboration with both of her scribes, it seems reasonable to suppose that she must have had a good working relationship with them. However, one correction that was made in two of Christine's manuscripts suggests that, with at least one of them, this might not have always been the case. In the Middle Ages, it was customary to signal the end of a text by writing an 'explicit' – for instance, 'explicit le *Livre du corps de policie*' means 'here ends the *Book of the Body Politic*'. On two occasions, the professional scribe who worked for Christine went a step further, writing their name and signing the work at the explicit. In both cases, the name was erased.[21] Although we will never know who performed this erasure, it is certainly plausible that, unhappy that the signature might allow the work to be attributed to someone else, the author did so herself. Christine's own name appears in the explicit of one work – *L'Epistre au dieu d'amours* (The Letter of the God of Love) – though somewhat unassertively, it appears in the form of an anagram, 'creintis'. This cannot therefore be called a 'signature', exactly – not least because the hand that wrote it is not in fact the author's. Could it be that Christine disliked the idea of signing her works? If so, perhaps her scribes decided to insert this signature in the form of a riddle – a small way of attempting to heighten their employer's importance.

Page written entirely in Christine's hand, adorned with her pen flourishes and a banderole around the first letter, folio from the *Avision*, 1410–15.

quilz soient prudens & bone vie
et preudomes ames quelle les
prenigne et se le contraire estoit
que tost ne les mette hors. Si
saura combien monte la despen
se de son hostel. Voudra savoir
ce que on aura pris des march.
& sus le peuple pour elle & pour
sa despense ordenera quil soit
bien paye a certain iour. Car
nullement ne voudra avoir
leurs maldicons nestre en le
bame. ne si ne voudra riens
devoir. mieulx ameia se pas
ser a moins & plus sobrement
despendre. Deffendra que on
ne prenigne riens sur le peuple
maltre eulx. et que ce ne soit
a iuste pris. et tantost paye/&
nomme faire aler les pouures
gens des villages et dailleurs
aleur grant coust destourbier
et fraiz cent foiz ou plus atout
une cedule en sa chambre aux
demeis ou a ses receueurs ains
quilz puisset estre paues. Elle
voudra point que ses tresoriers
ou distribueurs de ses biens
du stile comuny. Cest assavoir
soient menteurs. ne pour me
nans les gens de terme en ter

me. Ains leur ordenera qu
soient a chascun tel ter
come ilz pouront penser q
ilz puissent payer. Ceste
te dame ordenera la rou
ses revenues en la maniere
sensuit. elle le partira en
parties. La premiere sera
part et porcion quelle vou
mettre en aumosnes et do
aux poures. La seconde en
despense de son hostel la p
quelle saura quelle mont
re sil est ainsi que sur sa re
nue ou pension sa vie qu
et que son simple nesin a
mstieria sans quelle pe
le. La tierce. D apres
officiers & ses femmes/
te en dons a estrangiers
autres qui sui auront des
ptui ordinairement. Et
de somme mettra entre
Et la dessus prendra a sa
sance ce quelle voudra p
esse mettre en ioyaulx rob
et autres abillemens, et
chascune part et porcion
telle quantite come elle
ra quelle puisse faire su
sa revenue, et ainsi pa

ceste

On the whole, the door to Christine's scriptorium is forever closed to us, but occasionally, copies of her works afford us tiny glimpses into the processes that took place inside it and into the author's thought process as she compiled her works. Christine was herself not above making transcription errors, as can be seen from mistakes that have been corrected in her own hand. Such errors imply that she was probably copying from a master copy of her text, perhaps a personal copy that was kept in the workshop for this very purpose. The first folio of several works in 'The Queen's Manuscript' that begin on a new quire are quite dirty, the surface of the parchment tarnished and darkened from exposure to the sun and other elements.[22] This suggests that, once the text had been copied, its quires were left loose in the workshop for some time before being bound into a volume – painting the picture of a busy workshop with more than one project underway.

Sometimes, last-minute changes took place. The exact reasons as to why the *Epistre a la reine de France* (Epistle to the Queen of France) was effaced from folio 255 of 'The Queen's Manuscript', where traces of it can be seen, are unknown. One possibility is that, because it would have reminded her of unhappy events, the queen did not wish for this letter to be included in the collection. Because even the running title for the *Epistre* had been added to the page (usually one of the final stages of manuscript preparation), this change must have been made as the volume was nearing completion.[23] Elsewhere in the same volume, new lines were added where late additions needed to be made. Unlike the ruling of the rest of 'The Queen's Manuscript', which was done in a brown ink, these new lines are drawn in lead, giving them a distinctive grey colour.[24] Christine's scriptorium therefore seems to have had a flexible and adaptable approach to bookmaking. From all of

Page showing several corrections in Christine's hand, folio from *Le Livre des trois vertus*, c. 1405.

this, it comes across as a well-oiled and efficient enterprise that could cope with last-minute changes. It was a workshop run by skilled professionals, not amateurs who wished to try their hand at bookmaking.

Christine's Visual Enterprise

Because of the kind of evidence described, Christine is regarded not just as the editor and publisher of her works, but as an entrepreneur. Like all successful enterprisers, she knew the individuals who carried out tasks that she was unable to perform herself. The best evidence of this is found in a passage of *Le Livre de la cité des dames* (The Book of the City of Ladies) where Christine praises the work of a lady called Anastaise:

> On the subject of women who are expert in the art
> of painting, I know a woman right now by the name
> of Anastaise who is so talented and skilled in painting
> decorative borders on manuscripts and landscape
> backgrounds that one cannot find an artisan to equal
> her in the whole city of Paris, where the best in the
> world are found. She so excels at painting flower motifs
> in the most exquisite detail and is so highly esteemed
> that she is entrusted with the richest and most valuable
> manuscripts. I know this from my own experience,
> because she has done work for me that is considered
> exceptional among the decorations created by other
> artisans.[25]

While this passage is significant for its explicit testimony to the existence and great skill of female artisans, this alone is not all that remarkable since other sources attest to there being female artists in Paris at the time. However, few female illuminators and scribes are known by name, which sets Christine's testimony apart. The further significance of this passage is that it shows the extent of the author's involvement in the process of manuscript preparation. She did not just expect her pages to be decorated according to the fashions and conventions of the time, but sought out individual, skilled artists who had previously worked on volumes that were as precious as her own – a task in which she triumphed. In making the point that Anastaise worked on expensive volumes, Christine also subtly points out the worth of her own manuscripts.[26] Many art historians have tried their hand at identifying the work of this enigmatic Anastaise in Christine's manuscripts, but such attempts are doomed to failure. All that can be said for certain is that she must have worked for Christine before the author composed the *Cité* in around 1405, presumably creating the kinds of flower motifs the author praises in this passage. Several examples of this kind of illustration survive in Christine's manuscripts, but their designs are attributed to several different workshops. Although it cannot be known for certain which of these is the work of Anastaise, thanks to Christine's comments we know that at least one of them is the work of a female illuminator.

Although at first she was quite timid about asserting her identity, as she became more established in her career and her confidence as an author grew, Christine increasingly took pains to ensure that her name and authorship were known to readers. She did so by inserting her name into the titles of works, such as *L'Avision Cristine*, appearing as a protagonist within the narratives themselves, and, in particular, in ensuring that she was extensively represented within the visual programme of her manuscripts. Not all of Christine's manuscripts contain miniatures, though all bear some form of decoration – even if only delicate vine leaves or filigree motifs that climb up the borders of the page. That said, she was evidently keen to incorporate visual material into her manuscripts, since even her very earliest volumes contain images. Thirty-six of her 54 author-manuscripts were illuminated in a variety of Parisian workshops. This represents a significant amount of visual material, rendering Christine's one of the most heavily illustrated collections of work of the Middle Ages.

Over the course of her career, at least twelve different illuminators created images for Christine. Of these artists, the work of some (such as the Egerton Master and Ovide Moralisé Master) has survived in manuscripts outside of Christine's corpus – another sign that she enlisted professionals to illustrate her volumes. Yet this was not always the case. The Master of the First Epistle, whose name derives from *L'Epistre Othea* whose first iteration he illuminated, is one miniaturist whose craftmanship has not been seen outside Christine's body of work. For this reason, this unknown artist could have been one of her scribes, one of the women living in her household, or even Christine herself. As seductive as this last possibility might be, it is rather improbable, since the work of the artist in question shows a certain finesse that suggests it is the work of a professional artist, albeit one who was relatively inactive. Furthermore, since Christine was more than happy to admit the role that she took in penning her manuscripts, it seems unlikely that she would shy away from showing off her own artistic skills or those of members of her household. The Master of the First Epistle could have been known for working in other mediums, such as stained glass or canvas.[27] We cannot therefore draw any conclusions as to the professional status of this artist.

Although most of Christine's artists are anonymous, deductions can still be made about her working relationships with

Incomplete frontispiece marking the start of *Livre du chemin de long estude*, 1405–10. The decorative border could be the work of the enigmatic Anastaise.

62 0

7641

Tresexcellant maiefte redoubtee
Illustre honeur en dignite notee
Par la grace de dieu voiute digne
Congnoissant hileur on tout le mode encline
Tresdigne les haut ² marnifie
Pur ² denot de dieu fanctifie
Fil glorieux de qui vient toute fee
Bons tresque en prie ² crosse bid attrace
Dt hons hon roy de france redonbtable
Le hy charles du nom notable
Que dieu mantienne en iore ² en fante
Mon petit dit fort pumier presente
Tout ne fort il digne que tels mais aille
As aus hon houloir come hon fait me baille
Et prie a hons hane dues magnifies

some of them. As her career progressed, she developed an extremely fruitful collaboration with one particular illuminator, known now as the City of Ladies Master. Extensive work by this artist survives in other manuscripts, showing that, unlike the Master of the First Epistle, this was a highly skilled professional illuminator. Furthermore, the fact that he worked on many manuscripts intended for royal libraries suggests that he was an artist of some renown. Yet, although he was active for some time before he began to collaborate with Christine, that he derives his modern title from one of her texts, *La Cité des dames*, is testament to the importance of his work on her manuscripts.

The earliest work done by the City of Ladies Master for Christine dates to 1405, when he carried out three large, double-column miniatures in three of her manuscripts – one a copy of *La Cité des dames* and two volumes of its sequel, *Le Livre des trois vertus* (The Book of the Three Virtues). It seems Christine must have liked his illustration of the *Cité*, because over the next two years she asked him to paint the miniatures in two further copies of this text, extending its iconographic programme from one to three images – one at the start of each of its three sections. Save for a few minor details, the miniatures created by the City of Ladies Master are the same in all copies of the *Cité*. They are justifiably well-regarded by art historians: for a period when decorative arts showed little originality and largely replicated and copied pre-existing models, that the illuminations in *La Cité des dames* are not based on any precedent makes them refreshingly different.

Around the same time that Christine asked the City of Ladies Master to prepare the new iconographic programme for *La Cité des dames*, she entrusted him with another large project: to reproduce 101 illuminations for the copy of *L'Epistre Othea* destined for 'The Queen's Manuscript'. Presumably, it would have been cheaper and easier to ask one of the three masters who had already created the iconographic programme for a previous copy of the *Othea* to work on this second manuscript, so the fact that the City of Ladies Master was chosen seems indicative of a marked preference on Christine's part. Of course, it is possible that none of these masters were available at the time – none of them can be seen to have still been active when these illuminations were prepared. However, another factor that indicates Christine's preference for the City of Ladies Master is that, despite her having previously used so many different artists to decorate her manuscripts, with the exception of five miniatures for 'The Queen's Manuscript' which were carried out collaboratively, he is the only master to have worked on her projects after 1410. Even allowing for the fact that lost copies of Christine's works might alter this inference, she clearly increasingly used this particular master to carry out miniatures for her.

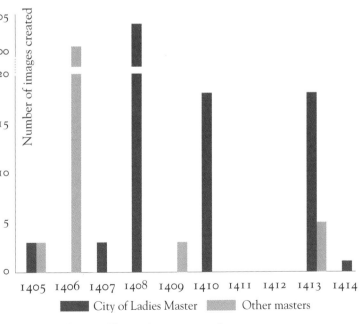

Artists working on Christine's manuscripts from 1405 to 1414.

Undoubtedly, there was much to recommend the City of Ladies Master. His colour scheme – which includes red vermilion, copper green, sunset pink and the deep shade of blue produced by lapis lazuli – offers a vibrant aesthetic palette. Especially when representing textiles, his drawings show a keen attention to detail. His faces are round, simple, open; his compositions airy, balanced and uncrowded. Although the backgrounds of his images are typically made up of a mosaic of tiny red, gold and blue squares, as in the frontispiece he created for the *Cité des dames*, at other times he paints a horizon that fades from blue to white in a way that is almost modern (see the illustration from the *Livre des fais d'armes et de chevalerie* in the next chapter). He is rightly regarded as one of the great masters of the period.[28]

One further aspect of the City of Ladies Master's artistry that is particular to his work on Christine's manuscripts, and that she must have found appealing, is the way in which he represents the author herself. Of all the masters to have worked on her manuscripts, he is the only one to represent her in a consistent and recognizable manner, which was sometimes copied by other masters. In each of his depictions of Christine, she wears a long blue gown with trailing sleeves and, on her head, a white, bi-horned wimple made up of several layers of white veils that extend around her neck. Although, to a modern reader, it may not seem so extraordinary for an author to be recognizable from their portrait, in the Middle Ages this was a novel concept. It was not until the very start of the fifteenth century that portraiture began to be used to create a recognizable representation of an individual. Until then, although portraits were intended to stand for a particular person, such representations were copied from generic models that did not tend to include distinguishing features by which an individual could be recognized. The City of Ladies Master was working for Christine just as the idea of true likeness in individual portraits was beginning to

Miniature of Christine instructing a group of men at the start of
the *Proverbes moraulx*, illustration carried out by the Bedford Master,
from *Collected Works* (The Book of the Queen), *c.* 1410–14.

emerge.[29] Although his portraits of Christine are still rather
generic – they do not show any individualized facial features,
for instance – they represent one of the earliest attempts to create
a recognizable and consistent portrait of a Western author.

While the mere fact of her works being identifiable by the
presence of a certain portrait would help to heighten Christine's
perceived importance, certain details of how she is represented
elevate her status even further. She is frequently represented
with books, for example, most often reading, writing or offering

one of her volumes to a patron, but sometimes also in a pose that shows her teaching. Of course, there was nothing unusual about depicting a writer with a book – in the absence of any other individualized or distinguishing feature, these common accessories have long been used in portraiture to signify that the person represented was an author of some kind, or to confer a certain amount of knowledge and authority on the individual in question. Yet portraits of Christine interacting with books do more than simply signify that she is a female author. The combination of her being a woman, holding or reading from a book, and of the deep blue of the dress in which the City of Ladies Master depicts her serves to associate her with a more powerful visual tradition altogether: representations of the Virgin Mary. Since the twelfth century the Virgin's blue gown had been one of her most common attributes.[30] Images of her holding a book were also one of the most popular ways of representing the Virgin, especially in small, portable prayer books intended for women and known as Books of Hours.[31] So, to anyone familiar with these depictions, representations of Christine created by the City of Ladies Master in which she wore blue and held a book inevitably called to mind the mother of God. Drawing on the model of the Virgin Mary also further emphasized and justified the position as a teacher that she often adopted in her works. It is therefore hardly surprising that such a depiction would have appealed to Christine or that she went on to entrust this master with further work. His author portraits only added to the authoritative status of his employer.

Another reason Christine would have liked the Marian connection made in the City of Ladies Master's representations is that it supplements an association made in her texts. Although Christine does not explicitly link herself and the Virgin, her powerful visual model, one that every reader would have recognized, enhances Christine's narratives and underscores her

political messages. In terms of the narrative, let us consider the
opening scene of the *Cité* (about which more will be said in
Chapter Three), where three virtuous women suddenly appear
to Christine and announce her destiny:

> We have come out of compassion to tell you about
> a certain building project in the shape of a strong,
> well-constructed city that you are destined to erect
> with our help and guidance and that will be inhabited
> only by illustrious, meritorious ladies.[32]

The arrival of the three women is preceded by a beam of light
that appears as if out of nowhere, shining onto Christine's lap.
As Jacqueline Cerquiglini-Toulet has pointed out, the detail of
the lap is rich in signification since it announces Christine's
maternity – a maternity which, in her case, leads to the birth of
a book. 'The Annunciation scene becomes for the poet a scene
of inspiration: the engendering of the book substitutes for the
engendering of Christ.'[33] Christine's fearful initial response also
echoes Mary's: 'terrified that it was some sort of apparition come
to tempt me, I made the sign of the cross on my forehead.'[34]
Annunciation scenes such as this, where individuals appear to
announce her destiny to the author, are encountered elsewhere
in Christine's works, notably in the *Dit de la rose* (Tale of the
Rose) and *Chemin de long estude*, although nowhere is the parallel between Christine and the Virgin made as clear as it is here.

Christine's use of the Virgin to add weight to her political
messages does not rely on imitation in quite the same way – not
least since the Virgin Mary did not have a political agenda as
such. She did, however, offer an ultimate example of a good
woman, one who could be entrusted with great responsibility.
Her divinity also made her a perfect entity towards whom
Christine's peaceful desires could be directed. In *L'Oroyson*

Nostre Dame (A Prayer to Our Lady), she repeatedly appeals to
the Virgin to grant 'peace and true tranquillity' to various individuals and in general.[35] But most of all, the fact that the Virgin
was a renowned and virtuous woman also made her an appropriate recipient for one of Christine's most ardent prayers, that
women should be protected from harm:

> Above all women, you come before grace: for the sake
> of the devout female sex, I pray you, take their bodies
> and souls into your holy care, whether they be young
> women, great ladies or others, protect them from
> defamation and do not let the fires of hell burn them.[36]

Although she was not a political figure in a traditional sense,
Christine uses the figure of the Virgin to support her own peaceful political aims. Yet Christine's appeals for peace had another
target: a woman who was herself a key player in the contemporary political scene, one who also used representations to
create a connection between herself and the Virgin: the queen,
Isabeau of Bavaria.

The event that is most emblematic of the association between
the Queen of France and the Queen of Heaven is Isabeau's coronation in Paris in August 1389, which was staged in such a
way as to create explicit parallels between the two women. The
date chosen was itself auspicious: it was the octave Sunday of
the Assumption of the Virgin Mary – the Sunday following the
feast of the Virgin's Assumption, a day that could be marked
with a second commemoration of the feast. So, Isabeau's entry
into Paris 'could be seen as a second commemoration of the
Virgin's Assumption'.[37] On that day, the heavily pregnant young
queen (she was to give birth to her first child just over two
months later) entered the city through a gate on the northern
perimeter, now the Porte Saint-Denis. As she crossed into the

city, two angels laid a crown on her head and proclaimed her
Queen of Paradise. Having made her procession through Paris,
she arrived at Notre-Dame cathedral. Here, the full significance
of the queen having been crowned by two people dressed as
angelic beings becomes apparent, since on its western facade,
the *porte rouge* bears a sculpture depicting the Virgin Mary's own
coronation by an angel. In the words of Tracy Adams,

> Isabeau's crowning by angels as she proceeded along the
> road that led her eventually to her coronation at Notre
> Dame would have created a particularly strong visual link
> between the physical Queen of France and the Virgin
> crowned by an angel on the portal of that cathedral.[38]

Around the corner, on the main, western facade, the Virgin
features once more, this time holding the Christ-child – the
result of her (and, by implication, the queen's) expectant preg-
nancy. According to the contemporary chronicler Jean Froissart,
later that day, those assembled at the cathedral sang 'high and
clearly in praise of God and the Virgin Mary'.[39] The assimilation
of the queen and of the Virgin was complete.

Christine's Scriptorium: At Best a Partial View

Try as we might to peer into Christine's scriptorium, its opera-
tions, artistic creativity and the interactions that took place
inside it will always be hidden from us. Nor are we ever likely
to have a complete inventory of all of the works that it produced.
That other copies of her texts have been lost can be conjectured
from inventories and various fragments, such as the single folio
of the *Cité des dames*, now held at the University Library in
Leiden, whose running head inscribed in red ink at the top of
the page indicates that this was once the 27th work in a much

larger manuscript.[40] Another of Christine's collected works manuscripts, known as 'The Duke's Manuscript', features the *Cité des dames* as the 26th item in the collection, and it is the 29th text in 'The Queen's Manuscript'. This suggests that the Leiden fragment was probably once part of a large anthology of Christine's collected works, possibly a volume that once belonged to Charles v's brother John of Berry, which is known to have been lost. The disappearance of this manuscript alone represents a significant loss. Gilbert Ouy, who devoted a large part of his career to Christine, has estimated that only around half of Christine's total output has survived.[41] Some losses, such as the removal of some of the illuminated folios from one manuscript (Paris, Bibliothèque Nationale de France, fr. MS 12279), might be less significant than the destruction or disappearance of complete anthologies or even entire works, but no matter how big or small, absences such as these irrevocably obscure our view of Christine's full literary and creative enterprise.

Another unfillable gap in our knowledge about Christine concerns how she acquired her knowledge of bookmaking practices and the book trade in general. But although such gaps can never be overcome, thanks to the collection of her manuscripts that have survived, more is known about her working practices than those of any other medieval author. Christine's controlling hand interceded in the careful creation of every aspect of her works – from the formatting of the page to the spelling, placement, size and content of the miniatures. Her approach allowed some of the finest examples of medieval artistry to be associated with her works and her active engagement with contemporary artistic and pictorial representations infused them with a rich network of significations.[42] In her hands, the simple act of offering a prayer to the Virgin became a discreet way of appealing to the queen to intercede in an increasingly desperate political situation. Christine's engagement in her own literary production ensured that the high quality of the finished product was appropriate for the patrons to whom they were intended while also bestowing a high cultural status on her creations. But above all, her involvement afforded Christine control over her own image. The awareness of traditional and new forms of representation displayed by one of the artists with whom she collaborated in particular created for Christine an innovative form of branding that portrayed her as a bold and authoritative writer – a boldness that is reflected in the confident tone of her works.

Christine in dialogue with the author Honorat Bouvet, illumination carried out by the City of Ladies Master, from *Livre des fais d'armes et de chevalerie*, 1410–11.

THREE

Christine Stems the Fountain of Misogyny

The names of countless authors . . . trickled into my mind
like drops from an endless fountain.
Le Livre de la cité des dames[1]

A lhough little can be said about Christine de Pizan's life
with any certainty, one thing that is demonstrably true
is that for a fifteenth-century woman, she was extremely
well read. This can be understood from explicit references
she makes to various authors and literary works in her own texts
and the many depictions of her reading, but also through details
that her own works share with others. On a surface level, the
form and plot of her texts and the characters within them betray
her deep familiarity with previous texts and with authors who
had also influenced her contemporaries. Christine was as knowledgeable about her contemporary literary climate as she was
about the artistic trade of medieval Paris. This enabled her to set
herself up as an authoritative and cultured writer and one who
could engage with points of contemporary debate that mattered
to her. In particular, she used her familiarity with previous texts
to wage war against the misogyny that was rife in many medieval
writings.

An Engaged Reader

Christine was not a passive recipient of the material she read, but a reader who actively engaged with her sources through her writing. Sometimes, her familiarity with past works can be seen in her reuse of their plot devices. For instance, the frame narrative of her *Livre du chemin de long estude* (Book of the Path of Long Study) is drawn directly from Boethius' *De consolatione philosophiae* (The Consolation of Philosophy). Both of these texts open with the protagonist, in each case a fictional double for the author, lamenting their condition: Boethius bemoans his state of imprisonment and Christine her constant misfortunes, beginning with the death of her husband. At the end of their lamentations, comfort is provided to each protagonist by a consolatory female figure: Lady Philosophy comes to Boethius, and a Sibyl (a character borrowed from Dante, who had in turn borrowed it from Virgil) visits Christine in her study. Christine is afforded a secondary source of comfort in the form of Boethius' work itself:

> I found a book which I loved very much, for it took me
> out of my state of dismay and desolation: it was Boethius's
> profitable and celebrated book, *On Consolation*. I then
> began to read, and as I read, the grief and pain that so
> weighed on me were dissipated.[2]

It should not come as a surprise that Christine names her source here, since she never sought to hide the influence of other authors on her own work.

Elsewhere, Christine engages with her past sources in a more intellectual manner, sometimes even going so far as to challenge them unreservedly – though she is more respectful of the works of some authors than others. One text she treats with some deference is Honorat Bovet's *Arbre des batailles* (Tree of Battles), one of the principal sources for her *Livre des fais d'armes et de chevalerie* (Book of the Deeds of Arms and of Chivalry). In the third part of Christine's text, a man appears to her in a dream. He tells Christine that he has 'come here to lend a hand in the composition of this present book of knighthood and deeds of arms'.[3] Although the man is not named, the rest of his speech makes it apparent that he is the author of the *Arbre des batailles*:

> It is good for you to gather from the Tree of Battles in my garden some fruit that will be of use to you, so that vigor and strength may grow within you to continue work on the weighty book. In order to build an edifice that reflects the writings of . . . authors who have been helpful to you, you must cut some branches of this tree, taking only the best, and with this timber you shall set the foundation of this edifice.[4]

In one of Christine's manuscripts, the ensuing exchange between Christine and Bouvet is illustrated, showing Christine literally cutting branches off the 'tree of battles' while its author speaks to her. This image accurately represents Christine's engagement with Bouvet's work: she cuts off bits of his text that she incorporates into her own, supplementing them with her own ideas where necessary. But although some of her exchanges with the author suggest that she does not always agree with his recommendations, she never directly challenges them.

When she disagreed with her source material, Christine was not always so respectful towards other authors, especially when it came to a matter that was very close to her heart, the subject of misogynistic attitudes towards women. In *Le Livre de la cité des dames* (The Book of the City of Ladies), the frame narrative is again inspired by Boethius: it too opens with Christine lamenting, only to be comforted this time by not one but three allegorical figures – Reason, Rectitude and Justice. The rest of the content of the *Cité* is largely inspired by another source, Boccaccio's *De mulieribus claris* (Of Noble Women). Unlike in the *Chemin*, however, reading does not offer Christine consolation in the *Cité*. Instead, it is the misogynist content of literature that provokes her unhappiness:

> Seated in my study as usual, I remembered that I meant to have a look at this book by Matheolus, so I started to read . . . The book's content did not seem very appealing unless you enjoy invective . . . It prompted in me an extraordinary thought: why is it that so many men – clerics as well as others – have always been so ready to say and write such abominable and hateful things about women and their nature?[5]

This reflection prompts the realization that 'I could hardly find a scholarly book, regardless of its author, that did not contain some chapters or lines criticizing women.'[6] From here, Christine develops a specific complaint around which the rest of the *Cité* will be formulated. Distraught, she continues:

> The names of countless authors who had written on this subject trickled into my mind like drops from an endless fountain. I concluded that God had created a vile creature when He fashioned woman . . . The idea of despising myself and the entire feminine sex as an aberration of nature made me deeply unhappy and discouraged.[7]

The image of the 'endless fountain' of misogynistic literature is supremely evocative, as it encapsulates both the sheer volume of writing against women that circulated in the later Middle Ages and the impossibility of stemming its flow. Just as water in a fountain never ceases to run, misogyny too only engenders the writing of more misogyny. Like a fountain, this type of discourse is also loud – it generates a volume so great that anything that might attempt to speak against it will be drowned out.

The topic of writing against women is a theme to which Christine returns in many of her works. In order to deflect the weight of the 'endless fountain' with which she is faced, she strikes out against its flow in different ways, sometimes outwardly criticizing misogynous works, sometimes interrogating them or engaging with them through dialogue. She makes use of the dialogic approach in the *Cité*, which is made up almost entirely of Christine's exchanges with three virtuous ladies. In the opening of this text, towards the end of her deploring the supposed nature of women, she laments: 'Alas, Lord, why did You not bring me into the world a male?'[8] It is this question that triggers the arrival of the three virtuous ladies, who set about answering this and all of Christine's subsequent questions. In answering her, the three ladies reassure the author that despite prevailing opinion tending towards the contrary, her own experience of women's good nature is perfectly valid. If anything, they claim it is more reliable since (unlike the male authors who denounce women in their writings), as a biological woman, Christine has first-hand experience of their goodness.

There is another purpose to the three ladies' visit: they bring news with them of Christine's destiny to build the City of Ladies. This City is, on one level, to be taken literally as a fortified city, a place in which virtuous women will be protected from the misogynous diatribes directed against them. As Reason says:

We wish to prevent others from making the same mistake you have made and to ensure that from now on, ladies

Miniatures of Christine and the three virtuous ladies (Reason,
Rectitude and Justice) in her study, and of Christine with Reason
building the City of Ladies, illumination carried out by the City
of Ladies Master, from *Collected Works* (The Book of the Queen),
c. 1410–14.

and all other worthy women will have a refuge and a
place where they can defend themselves from all these
assailants.[9]

The three ladies set about demonstrating women's good nature
by providing numerous examples of figures drawn from mythology, biblical sources and history. They include contemporary and
legendary women from saintly and noble backgrounds: Penelope
– Ulysses' wife, Dido, Jocasta, Medusa; the Virgin Mary and Mary
Magdalen; Esther, Ruth, Sarah, Rebecca; past and present queens
of France – Blanche of Castile, Clotilde and Isabeau of Bavaria.
Other notable contemporary and historical women include the
duchesses of Berry, Burgundy and Orleans, and the wives and
daughters of Julius Caesar and of Socrates. Each of these examples is cast as a metaphorical building block with which the edifice

of the 'city' is eventually built. To follow the building metaphor through, the city also operates as a double for Christine's book, since the various examples of 'good' women form the material substance of both. A further similarity lies in their function, since the book and the city are both created to contain the women and to defend them against misogyny. To underscore the building metaphor, Christine and the three virtuous ladies are shown physically building the city walls themselves in the illuminations – Christine applying a kind of cement with a trowel. The city is therefore built by women, for women and *of* women.

With the nature of these examples, we must return to Boccaccio. Not only is the form of Christine's text inspired by his work (both proceed by enumerating examples of women), but many of her exemplars are even drawn directly from it. This is not something that Christine attempts to hide, as she makes frequent mentions of Boccaccio's *Decameron*, as well as to another source that provides important material – Ovid's *Metamorphoses*. Demonstrating her profound familiarity with these works serves to bolster her own authority, as it shows that her own reasoning does not come from a place of ignorance. For a time, this familiarity with her sources afforded Christine criticisms of plagiarism: writing in 1922, Alfred Jeanroy accused Christine of 'unscrupulously pillaging Boccaccio's treatise, from which she drew . . . no less than three-quarters of her examples'.[10] However, such statements betray an ignorance of medieval compositional practices. Today's notions about the author being the originator of a new and original text did not exist in the Middle Ages, and works were appreciated precisely for being part of a network of material in which reliance on literary borrowings was perceived as a sign of sophistication.[11] Not only was such a practice commonplace, but it did not necessarily stifle originality: even those of Christine's works that draw most heavily on preceding texts innovate or respond to her sources in some way.

Traces of originality are often quite subtle. Although on first appearance the content and examples given in Christine's *Cité* are reminiscent of Boccaccio's *De mulieribus*, the overarching message in Christine's work is acutely pro-women, whereas many of Boccaccio's examples recycle the commonplaces of misogynous literature. His text therefore forms part of the endless fountain of misogyny that she criticizes. The example of Semiramis, the legendary queen of the Assyrian Empire, illustrates the different authors' approaches. While Boccaccio praises her many virtues, including her achievements as regent and conqueror, the fact that she married her son after the death of her first husband becomes a pretext for the Italian author to express a generalized misogynistic view that 'like others of her sex, this unhappy female was constantly burning with carnal desire, and it is believed that she gave herself to many men.'[12] Christine, however, omits Boccaccio's mentions of Semiramis' numerous lovers to focus instead on her military might. Towards the end of her chapter on Semiramis, although she does acknowledge the 'enormous transgression' that she performed in marrying her son, Christine justifies the queen's behaviour in saying that this was a political move to prevent another woman from claiming the crown. Christine also points out that, although her behaviour does not match the moral standards of the Middle Ages (or indeed of the modern period), it was not considered sinful in Semiramis' time and should not therefore be seen as grounds to exclude her from the city.

Boccaccio's 'famous women' are not therefore all positive examples. Indeed, many of the women whose stories he describes provide models for how *not* to behave rather than examples to emulate. He often contends that for them to be good, women must overcome their feminine nature – which is therefore implicitly bad. This is especially the case when it comes to learned women. Boccaccio writes of the Roman poetess Cornificia, for instance, that 'by means of talent and hard work, she succeeded in rising above her sex.'[13] What distinguishes Christine's text from Boccaccio's, and a charge that can fairly be laid at the doors of the *Cité*, is that hers sometimes celebrates the achievements of women to the point of bypassing their obvious flaws. There is a degree of truth to this, but it does not greatly diminish the overarching aim of Christine's text, which was to challenge the view of women in literature.

One area in which this can be seen is through the two authors' depictions of natural traits and behaviour: Boccaccio presents learned women as unnatural, since they had to reject their female nature to become so, whereas for Christine, it is the misogynist behaviour of men that is unnatural. As Reason declares in the *Cité*, 'any man who readily slanders women has a mean spirit, because he acts against reason and against nature.'[14] She goes on to say that some women have a great natural intelligence and can equal men in all subjects, from politics and government to philosophy and law. More will be said in the next chapter about the challenges presented by describing Christine as a feminist, but for now it suffices to say that she does not view women as being equal to men, but rather perceives each sex to have a fundamentally different set of characteristics. She believes, for instance, that men are naturally strong, whereas women are innately modest. Despite this essentialist view of gender, the important point for Christine is that modesty does not preclude women from being intelligent and, on that score, she sees them as entirely equal to men. Her own literary endeavours serve to confirm this point, since no figure better exemplifies a woman's natural inclination towards scholarly activities than Christine herself. After all, she used her learning and understanding to take on the great enterprise of creating the *Cité*, the work in which these views are being read! So, when engaging with previous literary sources, Christine has neither mechanically compiled and copied previous works, nor has she reproduced them uncritically. Rather, her process has involved holding previous literature to account by questioning and engaging with it on a more intellectual level.

In the examples considered so far, Christine has been seen interacting explicitly with the works of her predecessors by acknowledging and naming them, but her dialogic approach is not always so direct. Sometimes she favours a subtler, more implicit form of criticism that does not outwardly name and shame the texts to which she is responding. Christine employs both approaches in her engagements with one particular text, to which she returned at several points over her career and with which she took particular issue: *Le Roman de la rose* (The Romance of the Rose). This was arguably the text that had the most influence on cultural production in the Middle Ages and yet it was one of the most controversial texts of the period. To understand why Christine responded to the *Rose* as she did, it needs to be established how this became such an influential and controversial work.

Influence and Controversy: *Le Roman de la rose*

Composed between approximately 1230 and 1275 and standing at 22,000 lines in length, the *Roman de la rose* is a poem of epic proportions. Summarizing it is no easy task. On one level, it is a simple story of seduction: an unnamed male protagonist recounts a dream in which he falls in love with a rosebud (to be understood allegorically as a young woman). In his mission to seduce the flower, he is helped and hindered by a variety of allegorized personifications that stand for female attributes (with the likes of Abstinence and Modesty frustrating his efforts, and Beauty and Fair Welcome encouraging his advances). Personified allegories and dream narratives were both common tropes of medieval literature and so from such a description, the *Rose*'s plot might seem rather commonplace. Indeed, if the *Rose* had ended where its first author, Guillaume de Lorris, appears to have stopped writing it (after approximately 4,000 lines), it is unlikely to have been remembered as a significant work. However, some forty years after Guillaume's death, a second author, Jean de Meun, added a further 18,000 lines to the poem along with numerous complexities. Not only does his continuation bring the story to its natural conclusion (in which the metaphorical flower is plucked, standing for the penetration of the rose-maiden), but its narrative framework is vastly exploded. In Jean's part of the story, the allegorized personifications become ever more diverse, allowing him to expand the *Rose* into an encyclopaedic work that delves into philosophy and intellectual enquiry through the mouths of a vast cast of characters. Nature, for instance, whose monologue takes up some 4,000 lines, begins by lamenting the 'unnatural' behaviour of man and goes on to offer a discursive commentary on topics as varied as the nature of dreams, visions and free will, and the distinctions between humans and animals.

The popularity of the *Roman de la rose* in the Middle Ages can be seen from its survival in over three hundred manuscripts – an extraordinary number for a non-devotional medieval text. With the advent of printing, it enjoyed an equally remarkable print run, with over forty editions produced between 1480 and 1540. As such, it is not surprising that many medieval writers, including Christine, should have been influenced by this work. Many authors even mention it directly, although it was more common for the *Rose*'s influence to be felt more implicitly. For instance, several later writers reproduced its allegorical dream-vision format, including the fifteenth-century poet Jean Froissart, whose lover-protagonist in *Le Paradis d'amour* (The Paradise of Love) also converses with a variety of allegorical personifications who are also found within the *Rose*, such as Hope and Pleasure.[15]

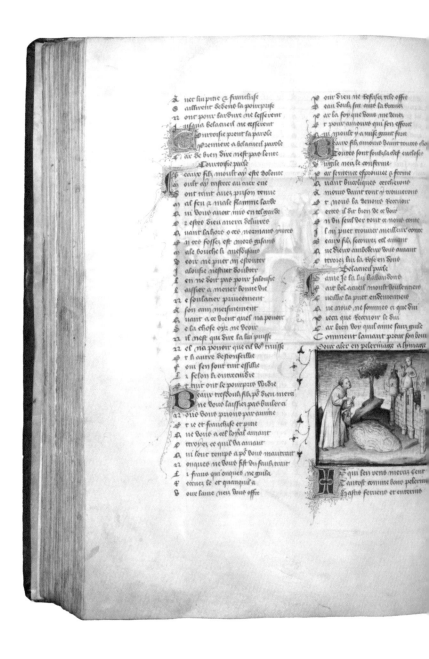

Miniature of the lover-pilgrim approaching the rose-maiden, folio from Guillaume de Lorris and Jean de Meun, *Le Roman de la rose*, c. 1410.

The *Rose* exerted a particularly strong influence on the fourteenth-century writer Guillaume de Machaut, in whose works it reverberates in various guises. The trajectory of seduction in his *Livre du voir dit* (Book of the True Poem) closely mirrors that of the *Rose*, following the five stages through which love progresses: sight, talk, touch, kiss and intercourse.[16] An explicit reference to the *Rose* appears in one of his debate poems, *Jugement dou Roy de Navarre* (Judgement of the King of Navarre), in which Guillaume de Lorris is even summoned so that one of the characters can challenge his ideas. The *Rose* is often cited in texts from the end of the medieval period as a valuable resource for readers who wish to learn about love. In René d'Anjou's *Livre du cuer d'amour espris* (Book of the Love-smitten Heart), the allegorized figure of Loyalty advises readers to read it to learn the commandments of the God of Love:

> Which, if you care to learn them,
> Take pains to read and look upon
> The most lovely *Roman de la rose*,
> There where the art of love is enclosed.[17]

Despite (or perhaps because of) its popularity, the *Rose* generated more than its fair share of controversy, due in no small part to its displays of misogyny. The *Rose*'s anti-feminine stance is evident both in the overall narrative of the poem, in which an active, male protagonist sets out to seduce a passive and objectified rose-maiden, and in the utterances of several of the characters. On this count, the Jealous Husband is one of the worst culprits. In a way that demonstrates the self-propagation of misogynous writings in action, the Husband, who is convinced that his wife is being unfaithful, backs up his own hatred of women by quoting the works of previous authors, lamenting that he had not paid attention to their teachings. He peppers the stream of abuse directed at his wife with references to, among others, Aristotle, Virgil and the Church Fathers – all of whom he claims had warned him about women. This is, of course, precisely the kind of recycled misogyny that Christine condemns in the *Cité* when she laments authors' continued propagation of the 'endless fountain' of anti-feminine writings. For the Jealous Husband, this body of literature is evidence not only of the whoreish behaviour and fickle nature of his wife, but of all women in general. He is given a voice for almost 1,000 lines, over the course of which he denounces women for their gossipy nature, their lying and their deceit. His speech concludes with the firing of a torrent of abuse at his wife that culminates in him viciously beating her. The following lines come towards the end of his diatribe:

> All of you women are, will be, and have been whores,
> in fact or in desire, for, whoever could eliminate the
> deed, no man can constrain desire. All women have
> the advantage of being mistresses of their desires.
> For no amount of beating or upbraiding can change
> your hearts, but the man who could change them
> would have lordship over your bodies.[18]

Closely related to the *Rose*'s misogyny is the matter of its distasteful ending. The narrative concludes with the storming of the castle that safeguards the rose-maiden and the eventual 'plucking' of the rose. At this point, the rose-maiden has been transformed into a statue that can just be glimpsed through the narrow aperture of a small window. So, to pass the guards undetected, the Lover approaches disguised as a pilgrim. He is attired in the standard pilgrimage garb of the time, accessorized with the customary long staff and leather pouch. The veil of metaphor at this point is extremely thin:

I set out like a good pilgrim, impatient, fervent, and
wholehearted, like a pure lover, on the voyage toward
the aperture, the goal of my pilgrimage. And I carried with
me, by great effort, the sack and the staff so stiff and strong
. . . The sack was well-made, of a supple skin without seam.
You should know that it was not empty: Nature, who gave
it to me, had cleverly forged two hammers with great care
at the same time that she first designed it . . . I believe that
she made them because she planned that I would shoe my
horses when I went wandering, as indeed I shall do if I may
have the possibility, for, thank God, I know how to forge.
I tell you truly that I count my two hammers and my sack
dearer than my citole or my harp.[19]

In order to obtain the rose-maiden, the pilgrim must insert his
shaft into the narrow opening between the two pillars that hold
up the statue.

This episode has been described as 'a barely disguised description of sexual intercourse, if not rape',[20] which is emphasized by
the rose-maiden's rigidity and lack of agency as a statue. Some of
the miniatures that illustrate this scene render it in a shockingly
explicit way, suggesting that even for a medieval audience, the
final scene must have been quite disturbing. Some manuscripts
depict the scene more candidly than others; the Valencia manuscript is one of the more explicit, representing the deflowering
almost cinegraphically over a series of images. The first miniature depicts the lover-pilgrim approaching the rose, his staff
suggestively protruding from between his legs. Meanwhile, the
statuesque form of the naked rose-maiden is provocative while
also stressing her powerlessness: the narrow window between her
legs forms a bawdy counterpart to the pilgrim's staff, and the rigidity of her legs, which are part of the castle walls, emphasize her
immobility. Her own desires and agency here have no place.

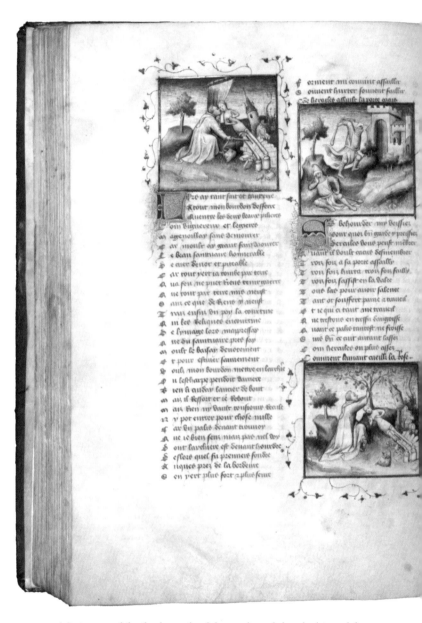

Miniatures of the final assault of the castle and the plucking of the rose, folio from Guillaume de Lorris and Jean de Meun, *Le Roman de la rose*, c. 1410.

Rooted to the spot, she awaits the lover's approach. The second image shows the act of plucking/penetration itself, as the pilgrim inserts his staff into the aperture between the motionless maiden's legs. Finally, in the third image, the act is complete; as a nod to the central metaphor of the narrative, the pilgrim plucks a flower from a rosebush above the maiden's body. Disturbingly, his shaft remains lodged in the aperture, while the rose-maiden herself looks shocked, though her pose is otherwise unaltered. The viewer of the images in this manuscript is moved to feel sympathy – empathy, even – for her. By contrast, in the text, the humour of the bawdy wordplay is privileged over any sympathy that might be felt towards the maiden.

Soon after this episode, the narrative is brought to an abrupt end, and no sooner has the rose been plucked than the narrator awakes.

Christine de Pizan's Responses to *Le Roman de la rose*

Even from this brief summary of the treatment of women in *Le Roman de la rose*, the reasons why Christine found this text so distasteful are easily apparent. Of all the texts that contributed towards the unstoppable flow of misogyny, none helped to justify anti-feminine attitudes in new generations of writers more than the *Rose*. It was precisely because of its popularity that Christine singled it out for condemnation. But a text that contains so much condemnable material requires several responses, which is precisely what she went on to compose. In some of her writings, she engaged with the *Rose* by directly commenting on the text, explicitly questioning it and stating her objections, but elsewhere she responded to it more subtly by composing material that only implicitly responded to some of its passages. Although modern readers may sympathize with her views concerning the misogyny of the text, some of her opinions – about its language, for instance – do read as puritanical and somewhat closed-minded.

One of the most striking features of the *Rose*'s misogyny is that the anti-feminine views it expresses are clearly addressed to a male reader – as can be understood from details such as the narrator's references to men with the pronoun 'we', for instance. It therefore represents the fountain of learned misogyny at work: a self-perpetuating torrent of literature written by and for other male clerics that drowns out any opposing views that might speak out against it. Women in the *Rose* are a subject to be discussed between men; they are themselves unable to respond to any of its views, or to challenge the ideology it presents. The *Rose* and its readers will remain fixed in an echo chamber of male voices that continues to reverberate misogyny. To counter this, Christine often responded to the *Rose* in an explicitly female voice; this is just one of the techniques that she adopted to stem the flow of misogyny.

Les Epistres sur le Rommant de la rose

Christine's most explicit response to the *Rose*, and the one in which she speaks most forthrightly in her own voice, comes in the form of a collection of letters that she gathered and entitled *Les Epistres sur le Rommant de la rose* (The Epistles on the Romance of the Rose) – a title that could not make the connection to the *Rose* any plainer. In it, the *Rose* is discussed head-on. The letters were not all written by her, however, but also by several leading scholars and intellectuals, many of whom sought to defend the *Rose*. Early in the fifteenth century, Christine entered into a contentious exchange with these men over the merits of this text. Although her correspondents formed intimidating and distinguished adversaries, she showed herself to be their more-than-worthy opponent. The anthology of letters that she assembled makes up what is sometimes referred to as the 'debate of the *Romance of the Rose*', the first recorded literary debate in French history.

The debate was triggered in around 1400, when a royal secretary, Jean de Montreuil, composed a short (now lost) treatise praising the *Rose*. About a year later, Christine wrote to Montreuil, criticizing his thesis and his position on the text in general. Although Montreuil himself is not known to have responded personally to Christine, two of his colleagues at the Chancellery, the brothers Gontier and Pierre Col, exchanged several letters with her. It is unclear why Montreuil did not reply to Christine. It is not impossible that he did, of course, and that this letter has not survived or that Christine chose not to include it in her collection. A less indulgent view is that Montreuil did not think that Christine – a woman and not a scholar – merited a response. This was certainly the view of Pierre Col, in whose letter it is evident that he reprimands her, a woman, for criticizing the works of 'Master Jean de Meun':

> You dare to judge, but yet speak only your own opinionated and impertinent presumptions. Oh, foolish presumption! Oh, uninformed words uttered too soon from the mouth of a woman, who dares to condemn a man of such high understanding, of such fervent study, who undertook such great labour as to produce such a noble book as that of the *Rose*.[21]

Not all of the letters that made up the debate were quite so cutting. In fact, the extravagant formulations of mutual respect displayed in most of them testify to the great esteem in which Christine was held by her contemporaries. Gontier Col directs his first letter 'to the prudent, honoured and learned Lady Christine', addressing her as a 'woman of high and elevated understanding, worthy of honour and great recommendation'.[22]

In return, Christine addresses him as 'most dear lord and master, holder of good morals, lover of science, most learned and expert rhetorician'.[23] Although such formalities of addresses are often found in exchanges between high-ranking people in the Middle Ages, their absence from later correspondence is notable, as it hints at the breakdown of that mutual respect. Pierre Col's final letter to Christine abruptly opens:

> Although you suggested that you would no more
> reprimand or accuse the . . . *Romance of the Rose* –
> a wise and enlightened stance by one who knows
> and understands that to err is human, but to persevere
> is the work of the devil – you will not prevent my quill
> from writing to you; for after so many accusations and
> responses on your part written against such a noble
> writer, my own righteousness and sense of ceremony
> force me to reply.[24]

For her part, Christine typically adopts a humble pose to return the compliments of her correspondents, though it too is occasionally tinged with a degree of sarcasm:

> I, Christine de Pizan, a woman of little intuition and
> of fickle understanding – for which your wisdom should
> not scorn my little knowledge, but might condescend
> to supplement my own feminine weakness.[25]

That Christine does not truly believe in the 'feminine weakness' she professes to have is evident in the vociferousness with which she goes on to defend her opinions.[26] In calling out her own weakness, she responds ironically to Gontier's amazement that a woman has engaged with the works of so many intellectuals, authors and poets. Is Gontier's amazement understandable?

On the one hand, it is unsurprising that he should admire a woman who has injected her own voice into a scholarly issue and formulated a coherent and convincing argument against a literary work. He can also be forgiven for being surprised to encounter a female correspondent: in the fifteenth century, it was hardly common for women to pen extended critiques of literary works and many of Christine's twenty-first-century admirers still hold her in high regard simply for the distinction of being a woman writer. A less indulgent view is that Gontier's amazement betrays his consternation at Christine's daring to intervene in matters that do not concern her. In choosing to engage with works that her detractors perceive as the preserve of intellectual spheres, Christine has transcended the boundaries set by her non-scholarly status and by her sex.

Christine sets out her objections to the *Rose* throughout her letters, and nowhere more succinctly than in her letter to Jean de Montreuil. As ever, her mind is firmly on instructional and educative goals and her various objections boil down to the fact that the work serves no practical purpose: 'this said work . . . should more rightly be called great idleness than useful, in my opinion.'[27] Not only that, but she accuses it of encouraging its readers towards actually doing more harm than good – notably in the lessons it gives on the treatment of women. Most disappointing for Christine is the fact that this is a missed opportunity: 'If only he had blamed the dishonest women and advised avoiding them, he would have provided a good and just lesson. But no! Without exception, he accuses them all.' Jean de Meun could have written a much better and more profitable work had he wished to do so.[28] Christine is not ignorant, and she does not deny that there are bad women in the world, but her problem with the *Rose* is that it implies that all women are such.

In her letters, Christine does more than just point out the *Rose*'s anti-feminine stance. She also humorously undermines it by pointing out the ridiculousness of some of its ideas. For instance, the *Rose* claims that women deceive men and force them to commit reprehensible acts, but how exactly are women able to deceive men, Christine asks? 'Do they come looking for you in your room? Do they beg you or take you by force?'[29] As a woman defending her sex, Christine is conscious that she leaves herself open to accusations of bias. She turns this to her advantage in pointing out that it is precisely because she *is* a woman that she is able to testify to the *Rose's* false representation of her sex:

> Do not think, dear sir, and let no one believe that
> I say these things to defend women because I am
> myself a woman: indeed, my only motivation is to
> defend the truth, which I know truthfully to be contrary
> to the things that have been said [in the *Rose*] which
> I deny; as I am truly a woman, I can attest to this better
> than he who has no such experience, but speaks only
> by guesswork and conjecture.[30]

Christine supplements this by indicating that Jean de Meun's knowledge and experience of women could only have been second-hand at best and must have been singularly poor. She points out that Jean accuses married women of having loose morals, yet he cannot have experienced this for himself, since as a cleric he was not permitted to marry. Christine says that for Jean to blame all women based on his experience of them, he must have only known 'dissolute women of sinful lives – as depraved men tend to do – and thereby got the idea, or he pretended to think that all women must be like that, as he did not know any who were not' – a not-too-subtle hint that Jean frequented prostitutes.[31] The personal response of a woman is therefore a valid counterpoint to any conjecture he could have put forward himself. By pointing out the ridiculousness of claims leveraged against all women, Christine has begun to take down one of the books whose anti-feminine message she laments in the opening of the *Cité des dames*.

Christine's objections to the *Rose* are not, however, limited to its misogyny. Although her condemnation of its anti-feminine message is understandable and her defence of women laudable, one of the points on which modern readers find it hardest to agree with her is the issue she takes with some of its language. Christine is particularly critical of the speech given by the character Lady Reason. In the passage in question, the Lover asks Reason for an example to illustrate her argument that love is superior to justice. Reason turns to the legend of Saturn, 'whose testicles Jupiter . . . cut off as though they were sausages and threw into the sea, thus giving birth to Venus'.[32] Christine's objection here is to the use of the word 'testicles' (*coilles* in Old French). But while her main problem with this word is that she believes it is used unnecessarily, she also takes exception to the fact that it is spoken by Lady Reason, who she claims would not use such unladylike language.

Whether or not this was her intention, Christine's objections and the defences made by her interlocutors mirror the dialogue that takes place between the Lover and Lady Reason in a subsequent passage of the *Rose*. The Lover chastises Reason:

> I do not consider you courteous when just now you named the testicles to me; they are not well thought of in the mouth of a courteous girl. I do not know how you, so wise and beautiful, dared name them, at least when you did not gloss the word with some courteous utterance, as an honest woman does in speaking of them.[33]

Pierre Col strongly objects to this point. Quoting Christine's argument at length, he goes into some detail to take down her

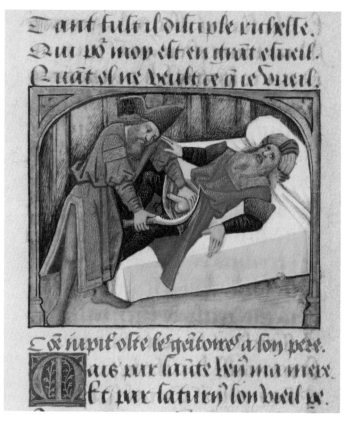

'The Castration of Saturn', miniature from Guillaume de Lorris and Jean de Meun, *Le Roman de la Rose*, 1475.

reasoning, claiming that the arguments of the fictional protagonist are superior to those of his correspondent.

Prudish though she may be concerning this first passage, it is easier to agree with Christine's argument that the word 'testicles' is used wantonly in the following, rather scandalous, extract:

> If . . . I had called testicles relics and had declared relics to be testicles, then you, who here criticize me and goad me on account of them, would reply that 'relics' was an ugly, base word. 'Testicles' is a good name and I like it, and so,

in faith, are 'testes' and 'penis.' I have hardly ever seen any
more beautiful.[34]

To say nothing of the shocking idea that the words for relics and
genitalia are interchangeable (if not the items themselves, as is
almost implied in this passage), one of the main problems here
is that by relishing speaking about male genitalia, Lady Reason
comes across as precisely the kind of shameless and lustful woman
that the *Rose* claims all women to be. Christine highlights that
the danger in having a reasonable female character using such
apparently harmless language is that it can be turned against
women and used to slander an entire sex. As she points out, the
confines of acceptable female behaviour are so narrow that what
might seem harmless can in fact provide fodder for misogyny.

The Wider Debate

In 1401 Christine began to compile the various documents
that had been written for or against the *Rose*. She later prepared
a copy of them to be included in a luxury manuscript of her
collected works intended for the Queen of France, Isabeau of
Bavaria. The collection of letters that have survived to this day
was curated by Christine, so we may therefore only have been
afforded a partial view of the full debate, the view that she wished
to give her public. The last letter in the collection, a lengthy
missive from Christine to Pierre Col dating to October 1402,
appears to be unanswered, but given that only a short amount
of time elapsed between the composition of the final letter and
the collection being put together as a gift for the queen (she
received it on 1 January 1403), further correspondence could
have ensued after this last letter was composed. Why go to such
lengths to disseminate these exchanges? For one thing, the fact
that the letters were deemed to be of interest to the Queen of

France shows the extent to which questions relative to the *Rose* were being discussed. The debate was not just concerned with the text, but 'extended to moral concerns on the role and function of literature in society'.[35] These concerns are often thought of as fundamentally modern, but the fact is, they also occupied the minds of the highest echelons of medieval Parisian society. In addition, the dialogue that Christine enters into with her contemporaries throughout the debate also served to bolster her reputation, allowing her to construct a persona for herself 'as an intellectual figure who participates in and controls a public debate that involved some of the preeminent intellectuals of her time' – so there was much to be gained for Christine, as well.[36]

A final point to be made about the transmission of the letters on the *Rose* is that they circulated beyond the small group of correspondents. This is evident from Gontier Col's first letter to Christine, as he requests a copy of the letter she sent to Jean de Montreuil. Clearly, he expects Christine to have kept copies of her own correspondence, as she would not otherwise have been able to supply one – nor would she have been able to include it in the collection that she eventually compiled. Jean de Montreuil must also have put the letter he had received into circulation, since otherwise his colleague would not have been able to read it. This is significant because it shows that the debate of the *Rose* was not a private affair between a few notable persons, but one that its participants intended for wider discussion. Determined to generate some public utility from her exchanges with her contemporaries, Christine took steps to make this dialogue public, thereby inviting future generations of readers to take part in the debate as well.

Christine was not the only one to take the discussion into the wider public sphere. In May 1402 the theologian Jean Gerson, chancellor of the University of Paris, published his 'Treatise against the *Romance of the Rose*'. Eight manuscripts of this treatise survive, suggesting that it too circulated relatively widely. Later that year, Gerson also delivered two public sermons against the *Rose*, bringing the argument to an even wider audience. By then, the debate must have been going on for some time. After all, the fact that Montreuil was motivated to compose a treatise in praise of the *Rose* suggests that there was already some debate surrounding this text. If the debate was ever to draw to a close, it would require an equally robust critique to be written in response, which is precisely what Christine offered in her letters on the *Rose*. She did not stop there, however. Christine offers a subtler, more implicit critique of the text in two shorter poetic works, *Le Dit de la rose* (The Tale of the Rose), and *L'Epistre au dieu d'amours* (The Letter of the God of Love).

Le Dit de la rose

Dated to 14 February 1401, St Valentine's Day, *Le Dit de la rose* tells the story of a gathering of nobles in Paris, to whose guests the God of Love charges Lady Loyalty to deliver a message. Loyalty says she has been sent to encourage those present to uphold the honour of women. To do so, she asks everyone in the audience to clasp one of the fresh roses she has brought from her garden. Together, those assembled swear that they will be loyal in love and defend women against anyone who should defame them. Taking this oath grants them membership of the 'Order of the Rose'. Christine, who once again features as a protagonist, is present at the gathering. When she retires to bed, Loyalty comes to her chamber with a set of additional instructions: she informs Christine that the God of Love is very upset by the conduct of men who defame women and whose gossip harms their reputations. She asks her to help put a stop to this behaviour by spreading the Order of the Rose, leaving her with an edict granting permission to do so, along with armfuls of fresh roses. Christine wakes up thinking the encounter was a dream, only to find the signed edict by her bed revealing that it was all true.

Unlike the *Epistres* that frequently refer directly to the *Rose*, the *Dit* never openly mentions this text. Yet the poem engages with this source in a variety of ways, notably in its cast of characters. Many of those in Christine's text originate from traditional sources, including the *Rose*, and are adapted to present the more equitable and respectful form of love that she advocates. The character of Lady Loyalty herself illustrates how Christine's vision of love differs from the *Rose's*: Christine's Loyalty is strongly associated with the God of Love, for whom she acts as a mouthpiece. This stands as a firm counterpoint to the *Rose*, where Love is instead paired with the inflammatory and destructive Venus – a character who is instrumental in helping the Lover obtain the rose-maiden, spurring him on with flames of desire.

Characters who feature in both the *Rose* and the *Dit de la rose* include the gods of Love, Envy and Courtesy. But although these three personages appear in both texts, Christine's borrowings do not extend to their characteristics, which are quite different to those displayed in the *Rose*. Christine's God of Love, for instance, is concerned with women's virtue and appeals to men to treat them with respect – quite a contrast to the inflammatory God of Love of the *Rose*, who pushes the Lover to ruthlessly pursue his beloved, no matter how forcibly she might object. Christine's adaptation of Envy is more akin to the characterization in the *Rose*, as both present this as a trait that is inimical to love. Yet, although there is nothing intrinsically misogynist about Envy in the *Rose*, for Christine this is precisely the emotion responsible for causing men to disrespect women:

> . . . that slandering
> (God curse it!) which dishonours scores
> Of women, wrongly, senselessly,
> And many worthy men as well . . .

That's Envy's work, who brings that dish
From Hell to serve it up above,
To poison everything about,
And bring a double death to him
Who's drawn to such malevolence.[37]

To stress the negative effects of Envy for women, Christine
contrasts it with Courtesy, another personification who appears
in the *Rose*, although her conduct in that text could hardly be
described as courteous. On the contrary, it is because of her that
the Lover is finally granted access to the rose-maiden who has
been locked away by her guardians in the castle. At the end of
the story, the God of Love and his army have defeated all of the
obstacles that lie in their way, and only Fair Welcoming remains.
Courtesy persuades him to let the Lover through, as a result of
which he finally succeeds in deflowering the rose. In the *Rose*,
Courtesy is a virtue whose excessive politeness goes on to facil-
itate precisely the opposite kind of behaviour to what her name
implies. By contrast, in Christine's story, she is written as a respectful, chivalrous virtue befitting of her name. Christine's Courtesy
makes noble men hold women in high regard – she is not an
attribute to be exploited to persuade women to sleep with them.

A final character who is altered in Christine's *Dit* is the rose-
maiden herself. In the earlier text, the rosebud stands for the
maiden's body and the plucking of the rose metaphorically stands
for sexual penetration. The *Dit* dismantles the rose metaphor,
replacing the literary conceit (in which the flower stands for a
maiden) with a literal idea and the flowers of fanciful allegory
with physical blossoms. The roses in Christine's text carry no
double entendre: they are 'gathered . . . in lovely orchards where
[Loyalty] tend[s] their growth';[38] their fragrant white and red
buds are placed in vases and made into garlands with which the
members of the gathering decorate themselves before leaving:

> . . . they bedeck themselves
> With roses – in their hair, their breast,
> Their arms . . .
> They begged their leave as they arose
> And carried off each valued rose.[39]

In Christine's text, there is no way of understanding the rose as a metaphor for a woman, or plucking as a euphemism for sex. Any metaphorical function the flower maintains serves to ally it with the virtue of loyalty, owing to its being the emblem of the new Order of the Rose whose purpose is to give women loyal lovers. There is likewise no innuendo to be read into the verb *cueillir* (to pluck), used three times in Christine's poem, whereas in the *Rose*, it is synonymous with sexual penetration. In the same way as in the *Dit* a rose is just a rose, plucking refers simply to the picking of a flower. Christine has in effect cleansed the rose metaphor: the layer of innuendo with which Jean infused the word has been extracted and it is now just a simple blossom.

That Christine is responding to the *Rose* in her *Dit* can also be seen in her choice of language, notably in her refashioning of some of its best-known lines. The *Rose* famously declares in its prologue:

> This is the *Romance of the Rose*
> In which the whole art of love is enclosed.[40]

These lines, and the rhyme *rose/enclose* in Old French, had been repeated in the works of numerous poets. Christine reproduces the rhyme in the *Dit de la rose* on two occasions. The first time it is used, it forms part of an appeal to the audience:

> Now he who will accept those terms
> And make that promise solemnly,

Let him boldly take the rose
In which all sweetness is enclosed.[41]

In its second occurrence, it forms a crossed rhyme in the three
final lines of the ballade that the audience recites as they join
the Order of the Rose:

Now lofty princes in whom worth inheres,
Recite the vow, where goodness is enclosed,
In many armies its standard I'll bear;
And thus I take the Order of the Rose.[42]

In Christine's text, the rose has not just lost its metaphorical
significance, but goes from emblematizing a form of love that has
harmful effects on women to being the ensign of two other qualities: those of sweetness and goodness. By repeating the *Rose's*
famous rhyme, now infused with pro-feminine associations, it
is clear that Christine was responding to these very lines – something that would not have been lost on her contemporary
audience.

Another famous passage from the opening of the *Rose* that
Christine adapts is one that contrasts dreams and lies through
the rhyme *songe/mençonge*. The opening lines of the *Rose* state
that 'many say that there is nothing in dreams (*songes*) but
fables and lies (*mençonges*) but one may have dreams which are
not deceitful, whose import becomes quite clear afterward.'[43]
Much ink has been spilled over these tantalizing lines, which
imply that the dream recounted in the narrative will reveal
itself to be true and that readers will be able to derive a clear
message from the text – neither of which prove to be the case.
Any anticipation that the cacophony of voices with which
readers are presented will eventually present a clear and
resounding message is left unmet.[44]

The opening of the *Rose* is recalled in the final lines of Christine's *Dit*, not only through the repetition of the rhyme *songe/mençonge* – a reuse of the rhyme that removes it from its original context – but in the way in which it engages with the theme of truth. Like the Lover in the *Rose*, the protagonist Christine wakes at the end of the *Dit*. She reflects on her encounter with Lady Loyalty:

> At first I thought it was a dream
> But then I knew it for no lie:
> I found the letter next to me,
> The one the sceptered
>   goddess placed
> Upon my bed, quite near my head,
> Who then departed through the air.[45]

At first glance, Christine says nothing different from the opening of the *Rose*: in both cases, the implication is that dreams can come true. But the key difference between the two texts is that although the *Rose* does not deliver any single 'true' message, Christine's poem concludes with proof of the truthfulness of her own vision in the form of the bull (sealed document) left by Lady Loyalty. This simultaneously underlines one of Christine's key arguments in her letters against the *Rose*, that Jean's text is full of lies, and proves the veracity of her own claims. Evidence of the truthfulness of her story can be found in the poem that Loyalty left for Christine, which readers have now seen and heard. Christine's *Dit* has thereby provided a truthful counterpoint to the *Rose*'s false and inadequate lessons. In rewriting some of its key verses, it enjoins readers to love and respect women.

L'Epistre au dieu d'amours

Christine's *Epistre au dieu d'amours* uses some of the same techniques as the *Dit* in responding to and undermining the *Rose*.
This poem takes the form of a letter penned by the God of Love
himself in response to complaints he has received from women
of all ranks about the way men have been treating them. French
men have been singled out as particular culprits, and so the
letter is addressed to the people of France in general. As in the
Dit, the mere fact that Christine's *Epistre* presents the view of
a God who speaks for and defends women, when a character
of the same name in the *Rose* was anything but pro-women,
demonstrates that this is a response to the earlier text. Like the
Dit, the *Epistre* also never directly mentions the earlier text. Yet
this second poem responds to the *Rose* subtly by humorously
undermining some of the claims it makes. In particular, it takes
the spotlight off women's actions, shining it firmly on male
behaviour instead.

The *Epistre* is one of Christine's sharpest, wittiest pieces of
writing. This is not to suggest that it will have readers laughing
out loud, but rather that the overall flavour of the text and the
ironic tone that Christine adopts is humorous. This is especially
evident in her description of the effects that love has on young
men's appearance and behaviour:

> They go declaring that a woman's love
> Inflames them sorely, keeps their hearts locked up;
> The first laments, the second's heart is wrenched,
> The next pretends to fill with tears, and sighs;
> Another claims to sicken horribly:
> Because of love's travail he's grown quite pale,
> Now perishing, now very nearly dead.
> Swearing their fervent oaths, they lie and vow

To be discreet and true, and then they crow.
Sparing themselves no pain to come and go,
They promenade in church and peer about,
Bending their knees upon the altar steps
In fake devotion: many are like that!
They spur their horses up and down the streets
Jaunty and handsome, jingling as they go.
They make a show of great activity . . .
Inquiring for the weddings and the feasts
At which those polished, ardent, gallant swains,
Display how much they feel our arrows' cut,
So much that they can barely stand the pain![46]

In this passage, Christine largely undermines the conduct of
male seducers by highlighting the commonplaces of romantic
language, especially the metaphors of fire and imprisonment
with which passion is frequently described in contemporary
poetry. She sarcastically refers to love's 'inflam[ing]' them and
'keep[ing] their hearts locked up', comments that become most
cutting when talking about the physical effects of love ('now
very nearly dead' and 'so much that they can barely stand the
pain!'). By quoting the tropes of love poetry in a different context, Christine can point out the ridiculousness of its exaggerated
claims. The great displays of professed affection and the language
used to seduce women are just another part of the spectacle that
she claims men put on to attract women. It is too melodramatic
to be serious. In reading this poem, it is important to remember that it would most likely have been recited aloud – one can
imagine this passage being delivered with some venom!

Christine also accuses men of lying, both overtly (through
calling out their 'fake devotion' and in references to pretence)
and in suggesting that their behaviour does not match the emotions they claim to be feeling – a charge that is tinged with

sarcasm. She takes this further by making fun of the behaviour of these false lovers. There is something very amusing about the description of the 'jaunty and handsome' young men 'jingling as they go' – which suggests they have added bells to their clothing in order to draw attention to themselves. Regrettably, none of the extant copies of this text were illustrated, since a portrait of the kind of gallant Christine had in mind would certainly add to the humour of the poem. Nonetheless, portraits of fashionable young men found in other works allow us to imagine the sort of ensemble she could have had in mind. There is a great deal of amusement to be found in the short tunics, tight trousers and long, pointed shoes worn by fashionable young men in the fifteenth century – costumes that were derided by contemporaries as well. By forcing her audiences to laugh at the appearance and conduct of such dandyish young fellows, Christine turns our attention away from any inappropriate behaviour on the part of the women and onto the conduct of the men.

In the *Epistre*, Christine also takes to task the harmful potential of male gossip on women's reputations. She claims that not only do men tend to exaggerate or lie about their exploits, but even if they are showing off about a seduction that really did take place, spreading stories about it can be very damaging. It is this kind of male banter, Christine claims, that harms women's reputations, not the actions of the women themselves. In other words, she does not condemn the relationship itself so much as the way in which it is discussed:

> Listen to how they make a game of it:
> Not satisfied with just betraying them,
> They've partners in their nasty liaison,
> . . . the less they got
> The more they boast of having been shut in
> The chambers of ladies who've loved them.

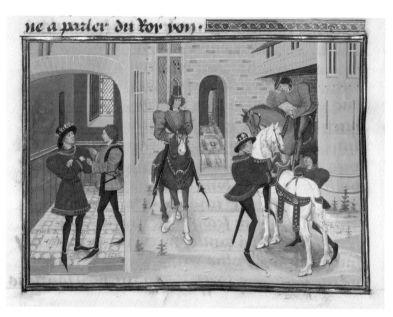

Miniature of a group of fashionable young men preparing
to go riding, from *Regnault de Montauban*, second half of
the 15th century.

They swear on soul and body how events
Turned out for them, and what the circumstance,
And claim that naked, arm in arm, they lay.
Their cohorts talk of it in every inn
And nobles share the news in huddled groups
In courts belonging to the dukes, our lords,
Or yet before the king, or elsewhere spread.
Of stuff like that their learned discourse comes!
Many of them should turn their talk instead
Toward telling fitting tales without bold lies,
Stories that show the worth of chivalry.
But lolling at those toasty evening fires,
They rib each other, and by means of taunts
Exchanged, they say: 'I know what you're about:
Your sweetheart's such a one, you play the beau

To have her love; but many get their part,
For you are greeted as another parts!'[47]

Significantly, this kind of gossip takes place in locations from
which noblewomen were excluded, such as pubs and taverns.
Christine also does not resist the opportunity to point the finger
at clerical education practices, suggesting that their teaching
serves merely to spread malicious gossip: 'of stuff like that their
learned discourse comes!' The way in which the men 'rib each
other' also shows the fountain of misogyny in action: in sharing
stories about their love affairs, even men who do not mean to
perpetuate anti-feminine discourse make comments that can be
extrapolated to imply women are by nature unfaithful. In teas-
ing men about having a disloyal lover (whether based on truth
or not), the ultimate victim is not just the woman involved but,
since this male banter engenders generalizations about the
female sex, extends to all women.

As entertaining as this might be, is this evidence sufficient
to warrant reading the *Epistre* as a criticism of the *Rose*? It could
simply be an opportunity for Christine to criticize misogynist
behaviour in general rather than an attack on the *Rose* itself.
She does not name the *Rose* directly in the *Epistre*, but she does
name one of its own principal sources, Ovid's *Remedia amoris*
(The Remedy of Love) – itself a text that engenders some
misogyny. Christine denounces the misogyny of Ovid's text itself
as well as the educational practices that taught it uncritically:

Now Ovid, in a book he wrote, sets down
Profuse affronts; I say that he did wrong.
He titled it *The Remedy for Love*,
And there he lays to women nasty ways,
Repulsive, sordid, filled with wickedness . . .
Now since their childhood days the clerks have read

> That book in grammar class, the subject that
> One studies first. They teach it to the rest
> In hopes they'll not seek out a woman's love.[48]

In other words, Ovid's *Remedia* has been selected as a text
through which young scholars will learn various subjects, including Latin grammar. But in reading a text that defames women,
students will also absorb different lessons from it. Such a practice
inevitably leads to the composition of further texts that exhibit
the same views. This would suggest that, to an extent, Jean de
Meun was not to blame for his anti-feminine claims: after all, he
had only been repeating what he had been taught as a student.
He had even anticipated that he might be criticized for some of
the views presented to his readers but defended himself by stating
that he was merely quoting what previous authors had written.[49]
By using such a technique, Jean was able to repeat the misogyny
of previous texts while simultaneously distancing himself from
it – although how convincingly he does so is open to debate.

Christine therefore does not just accuse the *Rose* or even Ovid
of propagating misogyny. But since the *Rose* was such an influential work and one of the texts that Christine explicitly singles out
as perpetrating – and even legitimizing – bad behaviour towards
women, she does not simply attack it, but goes further back to
target its own sources and specifically the clerical practices that
enabled such views to exist. These practices are the pump that
keeps the waters of the fountain of misogyny flowing. Christine's
lament in the opening of the *Cité* shows that she was deeply
troubled by the misogynist messages she saw emanating from all
literature. The *Rose* was just another text in a long line of works
that propagated and encouraged behaviour that was damaging
towards women. To stem the flow of anti-feminine literature
that derived from it would be to block one of the main streams
that continued to feed the 'endless fountain' of misogyny.

Stemming the Fountain of Misogyny

Reciting and responding to other texts was a common compositional and cultural practice in the Middle Ages – one that Christine often made use of in her own works. But though she partook of this practice, Christine shows that doing so unreservedly can lead to the repetition of deceitful ideas and misinformation as if they were fact. Instead of unquestioningly repeating what previous authors have said, Christine proposes an alternative practice: leading by example, she shows that it is possible to actively engage with contemporary and previous culture by challenging, not recycling, received ideas. In this way, each author can add nuance to previous texts rather than mechanically repeating them. But Christine is far from implying that authors should not be inspired by previous works – the form and content of her texts show that she drew on numerous sources when composing her own. What she does maintain, however, is that writers should challenge those sources as they have a moral duty to correct lazy or unsubstantiated views that could be detrimental to society. By disclosing the misogyny of anti-feminine writings, she encourages authors to take a more creative and intellectual approach to their own work and to consider which ideologies they wish to perpetuate. Challenging the status quo does not mean being unable to produce cultural artefacts; it means innovating within that culture and enabling it to change. Only in this way could the endless fountain of misogyny finally be stemmed.

Dedication scene from Christine's *L'Epistre Othéa*,
second half of the 15th century.

FOUR

Christine's Legacy in Early Modern and Modern Culture

You among all women have been given the privilege to build
the City of Ladies . . . Your city will be beautiful beyond
compare and it will last forever.
Le Livre de la cité des dames[1]

After her death in around 1431, Christine de Pizan endured a multifaceted future. Like many medieval authors, at the dawn of the Renaissance she fell into relative obscurity as new writers and thinkers sought to distance themselves from what were already termed the 'Dark Ages'. Although some authors, including Christine, were remembered for a short time, a veil of obscurity was gradually cast over the cultural and scientific advances represented by the thousand-year period of the Middle Ages.[2] Although transitions between periods are always quite arbitrary, the one between the medieval and the early modern eras was solidified by an innovation that revolutionized the manufacture of textual and artistic cultural artefacts: Gutenberg's invention of printing with moveable type in the 1450s. From this time onwards, texts no longer needed to be laboriously written out by hand one at a time, as multiple identical copies or editions could now be printed in a fraction of the time it had taken to copy a single manuscript. This not only made books cheaper, but increased their accessibility and made them available to different markets. However, the transition from hand-copied to typeset documents did not take place over-night. The demand for handwritten manuscripts continued into the late fifteenth century and illuminators continued to paint individual miniatures and initials for manuscripts and printed books for several more centuries.

The last manuscript written in Christine's hand dates to 1429 and it is assumed that she must have died within a year or two of this date – she would by then have been in her mid-sixties, a very good age for a woman in the fifteenth century. Although she was no longer around to personally oversee her literary pro-duction, several editors and translators soon took on this task, ensuring that some of her works were read into the sixteenth century. For a time, her name was also passed down in the writ-ings of various poets and historians, who ensured it some small survival, until her works were fully rediscovered in the nine-teenth century. Christine was one of several medieval authors to re-emerge thanks to (or perhaps because of) the fascination that the Middle Ages held for leading figures of the Romantic movement. In France, the likes of Chateaubriand and Victor Hugo were captivated by the idealized mysticism of a pre-industrial period and intrigued by the focus on nature and individual heroic feats described in certain strands of medieval literature (William Blake and John Keats maintained similar fascinations in England). Suddenly, in the 1800s, the Middle Ages were fashionable again. Having spent hundreds of years gathering dust, manuscripts that told of knightly adventures, sung of love potions and depicted magical beings were taken back off the shelves, allowing their stories to be told once more.

Had it not been for this revival of interest in the Middle Ages, Christine's works might still be mouldering away in var-ious archives, rather than prized as the treasures that they are today. After the Romantic revival saw new editions of her works being published, Christine then underwent a significant feminist revival that started in the late nineteenth century and has since gained more traction, leading her to become a source of inspiration to early twenty-first-century artists.

On the Brink of Oblivion in the Early Modern Period

During her lifetime and in the decades following her death, manuscripts of Christine's works continued to be copied by various scribes. Over 150 further manuscripts of her texts were made from those she had produced herself. With the advent of printing, multiple editions of her texts followed, with at least eighteen editions of her individual works published between 1450 and 1549. In manuscript and print form, her works were transmitted across Europe, with some even translated into Dutch, English and Portuguese. As for Christine's poetic reputation, her place in the literary canon was assured by the generation of French poets that followed her, as celebrated writers went on to praise her skill in their own writings. In his *Champion des dames* (Champion of Ladies) of around 1441, Martin le Franc says we should not forget

> . . . valiant Christine
> Whose virtue is manifest
> Both in French and in Latin.
> Her works and her poems
> Should not be covered up
> Such that, though death shrouds
> The body, her name lasts forever.[3]

On the other side of the Channel, the poet Thomas Hoccleve had already used her *Epistre au dieu d'amours* (Letter of the God of Love) as the basis for his own *Letter of Cupid* of 1402, translating large passages of the French text, though without mention of Christine, and all the while adapting it into an altogether different work.[4]

But as this last example shows, while her works enjoyed a certain acclaim among readers and audiences, even forming the inspiration for new ones to be composed, Christine herself was paradoxically largely being erased from literary history. As the memory of her faded, copies of her texts either went on to circulate anonymously or were attributed to male writers. Since the names of many medieval authors were often replaced by the name of the editor when they were printed, this is not necessarily indicative of historical sexism. However, the types of changes that took place in printed editions of Christine's texts do reflect an attempt to erase the sex of the original author. A case in point is her *Livre des fais d'armes et de chevalerie* (Book of the Deeds of Arms and of Chivalry) – a manual on medieval warfare. In Antoine Vérard's edition of 1488, it was attributed to one of her principal sources, the Roman writer Vegetius.[5] Although Vérard might be forgiven for confusing an author with their source, or for assuming that a book on warfare was unlikely to have been written by a woman, the fact that it references several medieval sources prevents it from being the work of a fourth-century author. A publisher as prolific and knowledgeable as Vérard would have known full well that Vegetius had not composed the *Fais d'armes*. The changes brought about by the scribe Jean Miélot, who produced two sumptuously illustrated manuscript copies of Christine's *L'Epistre Othea* (The Epistle of Othea) between approximately 1455 and 1460, are even less justifiable. Miélot not only took the author's place in the dedication scene of one of the manuscripts he prepared (though, curiously, not both) but the lengthy additions he provided to Christine's text suggest he tried to make up for some of its perceived deficiencies.[6] Miélot was not the only one to remove traces of Christine: several printed editions of the *Othea* were anonymized and manuscripts sometimes featured a male author in the dedication scene, replacing the female writer shown in Christine's manuscripts.

However, details of Christine's authorship were not always erased in the early modern period. Although her name tended to be dropped from French editions and copies of her works, English printers seem to have maintained a particular fascination with the novelty of a woman writer – especially one from the enemy court of France. Collectively, they translated five of her works, which were published in several editions between around 1450 and 1545. By comparison, French publishers did not show any interest in Christine until 1488, and only three of her texts survive in French early printed editions. But, in the years that immediately followed her death, although the advent of printing had enabled some of Christine's works to enjoy a wider readership, their author was herself slowly being forgotten. Where her authorship was not removed entirely, portraits and title pages in editions of her texts reveal some confusion as to her gender and identity. Certain biographers masculinized her name as 'Christinus de Pisis' and others claimed her son had composed the texts attributed to her.[7] Writing in the eighteenth century, the philosopher Voltaire mistakenly cites her name as 'Catherine'.[8] Stephen Scrope, a fifteenth-century translator of the *Othea*, confuses her identity as a patron who had ordered others to compile the text for her: 'This said book, at the request and prayer of a very wise gentlewoman of France called Dame Cristine, was compiled and created by the famous doctors of the most excellent in clergy at the noble University of Paris.'[9] Another fifteenth-century Englishman, William Worcester, who translated the *Fais d'armes* for the printer William Caxton, similarly casts Christine as 'a famous lady who was born, died, and lived in a religious house in Poissy' – biographical confusion that may have arisen from Christine's *Dit de Poissy* (Tale of Poissy), in which she describes visiting her daughter who had taken the veil at the abbey of Poissy near Paris.[10]

Over the course of the next few centuries, Christine's name
and her works continued a steady descent into relative oblivion,
although in the ensuing years her name was not entirely forgotten – Earl Jeffrey Richards has uncovered over fifty mentions of
her between 1545 and 1795.[11] However, after 1549 there was
not a single edition of her works until 1838. During this period,
however, few people could have actually read her works because
they simply were not in circulation. For over two centuries, since
no modern editions had yet been prepared, only specialists who
had access to (and were able to decipher) medieval manuscripts,
or those with access to archival material, were able to read
Christine's texts. If her name survived, it was largely thanks to
her biography of Charles v, *Le Livre des fais et bonnes meurs du
sage roy Charles v* (The Book of the Deeds and Good Conduct
of the Wise King Charles v), which continued to be referenced
by some historians. Excerpts of it were even printed by monar-
chists in the run-up to the French Revolution of 1789, suggesting
the text circulated in some form at the time.[12]

One specialist who did engage with Christine's biography in
this period was the eighteenth-century scholar Jean-Marie-Louis
Coupé. In a lengthy article that appeared in 1779, he creatively
extrapolates a love affair between Christine and one of her
patrons, the Englishman John Montagu, Earl of Salisbury. In
Coupé's essay, Christine – of whose physical appearance no contemporary description survives – is imagined as a woman whose
beauty matched her talents: 'but if her skill had already earned
her many admirers, her beauty procured her even more slaves.'[13]
'Her beauty', writes Coupé, 'was another burden, that kindled
a thousand passions which added greatly to her troubles.'[14] He
even goes so far as to compose dialogue between Christine and
Salisbury. A short excerpt suffices to illustrate the saccharine
tone of the piece:

'Merciful knight', she said to him, 'lover of poetry – yourself a beguiling poet, would you not yourself grace my ears with some gentle song?'

'Oh you, the pearl of the highest minds', he answered, 'most beautiful flower; since you have sung, no more can I sing. Oh my heart's desire, delight of my eyes, tormentor of my mind . . .'[15]

There is little basis for Coupé's fabrications. Christine wrote fondly of Salisbury in *Le Livre de l'avision Cristine* (The Book of Christine's Vision) and in ballade 22 of her *Autres balades* (Other Ballades), because he had arranged for her eldest son, Jean de Castel, to live in England as a companion for his own. Elsewhere in the *Avision*, she writes of her affliction that rumours had circulated about her involvement with a man, though she does not give any clues as to the identity of the supposed suitor. In any case, it is unlikely to have been Salisbury himself, since he only stayed a brief time in Paris.[16] The romantic liaison between Salisbury and Christine is therefore entirely a concoction of Coupé's, contrived from two unrelated details from her biography. It had some impact, nonetheless: the English author Horace Walpole was so taken with the story that he asked a friend to procure a copy of the portrait of the lady who had so beguiled the English aristocrat.[17]

Although these few references kept Christine's name from sliding into total obscurity, the medieval author's works had no more than a little impact on early modern culture. The rediscovery and widespread publication of her works in the nineteenth century enabled a legacy to be formed around her. Her popularity went on to be amplified to such a degree that, by the turn of the twenty-first century, the rate at which her works were being read and her impact on artistic creations were beyond anything she could have imagined 650 years earlier.

Christine's Twentieth-century Feminist Rebranding

In Simone de Beauvoir's major feminist treatise of 1949, *Le Deuxième sexe* (The Second Sex), the French philosopher singled out Christine as the first woman to 'take up her pen in defense of her sex', praising the 'lively attack on the clerics in her *Épître au dieu d'amour*' that she had initiated.[18] Until the first article on Christine as a defender of her sex was published in 1886, any interest in her had largely ignored the pro-feminine message put forward in so many of her works.[19] Between then and the publication of Beauvoir's treatise, a small flurry of studies and articles on the medieval author's pro-feminine stance had followed – seventeen in total. These were written in English, French and German – a testament to the interest in Christine outside her adoptive country. The first book-length analysis of Christine's feminism was Rose Rigaud's *Les Idées féministes de Christine de Pisan* of 1911.

Although, as has often been thought, Beauvoir was not therefore the first to discuss Christine's proto-feminism (which is to say that she displayed some ideas in common with feminism without being a feminist, as such), she can be credited with bringing Christine's name into the mainstream: before then, she had only featured in the works of specialist scholars and historians. Beauvoir mentions her alongside the ancient Greek poet Sappho, whose poetry is remembered for its celebration of female sexuality, including same-sex love, and Mary Wollstonecraft, the advocate for women's rights and author of *A Vindication of the Rights of Woman*. Beauvoir herself was writing against the backdrop of the women's suffrage movement – women had only been granted the vote in France in 1944. Yet she does not label Christine a feminist. To do so would be anachronistic since the term 'feminism' was not coined until the mid-nineteenth century and the notion of female equality was non-existent in the Middle Ages.

However, some of what Christine advocates in her writings *is* in harmony with the aims of modern-day feminists. She demands that women be treated respectfully, for instance, endorses the education of girls and champions financial protection for widows. Yet she never argues that women are equal to men. On the contrary, in *Le Livre des trois vertus* (The Book of the Three Virtues), she tells women in no uncertain terms to 'obey [their husbands] without complaint'.[20] In the same text, she advises women to turn a blind eye to their husbands' infidelities and to any 'perverse and rude behaviour' because 'you must live and die with him whatever he is like.'[21] Christine anticipates that some readers might object on the grounds that it is the badly behaved husbands who are in need of instruction rather than their wives. In response, she states that although 'it is well known that there are some husbands who behave very distantly towards their wives and give no sign of love, or very little . . . our teaching in this present work is not addressed to men'.[22] In other words, although husbands undoubtedly should treat their spouses better, Christine's concern is to give their wives coping mechanisms to help manage the difficult situations that marriage inflicts on so many of them. The purpose of the *Trois vertus* is to recognize those difficulties and provide women with practical advice to help them cope. Although her concern with improving the lot of women is one that Christine shares with modern feminists, because her views do not approximate to equality between the sexes, her works should only be considered pro-feminine (in other words, pro-women) or proto-feminist at best.

Some feminist critics have not been so indulgent of this aspect of Christine's writings, sometimes going so far as to label certain of her claims as downright anti-feminist. Sheila Delany is one who pulls no punches:

> I have been angered by Christine's self-righteousness,
> her prudery, and the intensely self-serving narrowness
> of her views. I have been repulsed by the backwardness
> of her social attitudes, attitudes already obsolescent in the
> early fifteenth century when Christine lived and wrote.[23]

One of the criticisms that Delany levies against Christine is that her advice focuses on the upper echelons of society – in particular the nobility. It should be remembered, however, that this is precisely the audience for whom Christine was writing. Not only had members of the nobility commissioned many of her texts, but in the early fifteenth century books were generally beyond the means of anyone who ranked below the upper bourgeoisie, and the idea of writing conduct books for a working-class audience (a type of book that was inherently aristocratic) would have been absurd. To Christine's credit, part of what distinguishes the *Trois vertus* from other medieval conduct books is that it does at least include advice that concerns working-class women, even if it is not directed to them.[24] Although this text largely addresses noble women, Christine enjoins her readers to provide good treatment and protection towards those whose conditions are beneath their own. Despite its shortcomings, some of its guidance is very inclusive. For instance, one chapter encourages women to familiarize themselves with their husbands' business so that they can operate independently – advice that stands for women of all classes.[25]

Regardless of whether she deserves to be labelled a feminist or not, Christine's rediscovery has earned her a large twentieth- and twenty-first-century fanbase that she is unlikely to lose any time soon. Editions and translations of her texts have multiplied in recent decades and made their way onto university reading lists around the world, leading to several of them now being available in inexpensive paperback editions. Her pro-feminine texts continue to be the most popular and none more so than *Le Livre de la cité des dames* (The Book of the City of Ladies). Since its first modern publication in the 1980s, this text has been translated into six different languages, adapted into a five-part series for BBC radio,[26] formed the basis for the theatrical performance *Je Christine* by the American actress Suzanne Savoy, and been reincarnated as a beautifully illustrated Italian children's book that is currently on its sixth reprint.[27] The fact that the 1982 English translation was reviewed in publications such as *Ms. Magazine*, the *New York Times* and *The Observer* marks Christine's entry into mainstream modern culture.[28] The old French edition of the same text has now been printed five times.[29]

It is the unfortunate case that many women in the public eye who express feminist views face a misogynistic backlash. Christine has not been immune from such censure. Misogynistic treatments of the author are far outnumbered by the voices that celebrate her, but one critical opinion that stands out is that of the prominent French literary historian Gustave Lanson. Lanson explained his reasons for excluding Christine from his *Histoire de la littérature française* (History of French Literature) of 1894 in the most condescendingly misogynistic terms:

> We will not stop to consider the excellent Christine de Pizan, a good girl, good wife, good mother and moreover one of the most veritable bluestockings to be found in our literature, the first of that insufferable lineage of women authors . . . who . . . have no concern but to multiply the proof of their tireless facility, equal to their universal mediocrity.[30]

An altogether different brand of anti-feminism is to be found in one of Christine's most recent incarnations in popular culture, as a character in the video game *Bladestorm: The Hundred Years'*

War (2007). Although in this game she is cast as a 'scholar', her credentials in that field are far from being on show. For the creators of this game, a medieval female scholar equates to seduction and witchcraft. The character Christine de Pizan appears in a mission where she entrusts the player with specific tasks: to collect precise forms of wood and iron, and to protect her while she searches for sulphur – ingredients she needs to make spells. Although this apparent confounding of Christine's scholarly credentials with witchcraft is regrettable in and of itself, as is the fact that she is an entirely ineffective fighter who regularly misses her targets – which she does while taunting the player's own moves in an exaggerated and syrupy French accent – it is in her attire that she is most different from her representation in her works. Gone are the simple gown, the wimple, the multiple layers of veils that she wears in her manuscripts. In their place, *Bladestorm*'s Christine wears a tight pink dress made up of two panels of fabric whose sides are just barely stitched together. Her large breasts spill out from the side of the halterneck bodice and her skirt is split open to reveal stockings held up by frilly garters. This outfit is accessorized with high-heeled platform shoes, a tall, purple, fez-like hat and a pair of spectacles that perch coquettishly on her nose. Fortunately, representations such as this are few and far between. Although it is hardly unusual for a female character in a video game to be sexualized, it is nonetheless regrettable that some gamers will encounter the

Christine de Pizan as a character in the videogames *Bladestorm: The Hundred Years' War* (2007) and *Bladestorm: Nightmare* (2015).

fifteenth-century author not as a learned woman of letters, but as a sex-kitten-cum-sorceress. For Christine to have been recast in this light entirely obscures her pro-feminine views. Anyone familiar with her reputation or writings might see her sexualization and the silencing of her pro-feminine views as punitive, even – it is almost as if she has been redesigned in such an objective way in retaliation for having dared to speak out for women. *Bladestorm*'s Christine is no longer a proto-feminist entrepreneur and writer, but an object of frustrated desire for an implicitly male player that conforms to a sexualized stereotype.

As a modern feminist champion, Christine therefore remains a controversial and ambivalent figure. Yet this remains a central part of her legacy for modern audiences. Few of her writings currently enjoy the same popularity as the *Cité des dames*: the French text of the *Fais d'armes*, one of her most successful works with early modern audiences, has so far only been edited as part of a PhD dissertation, although a new edition is in the works. Her lyric poetry, held in such high esteem by the generation that followed Christine's own, and her devotional writings, are largely ignored by modern readers.

Nevertheless, the significance of her works was recognized in 2017 when her *Livre du duc des vrais amans* (Book of the Duke of True Lovers) was included as a set text for the *agrégation de lettres modernes* – a prestigious and competitive examination that must be undertaken by those wishing to teach in further education in France. Its syllabus is largely seen as determining the French literary canon and it has a significant impact on publishing. *Le Duc des vrais amans* in many ways epitomizes the themes and characteristics of Christine's writing. Although, on the surface, it is a simple story of a failed aristocratic love affair, in its narrative Christine also distances herself from a conventional story to offer a moral tale about the risks to which romantic indiscretions expose women. In terms of its form, it

is mostly composed in prose with poetic and epistolary inser-
tions – examples of Christine's dexterity with different modes
of writing that can be seen in her collections of lyric poetry
and her letters on the *Roman de la rose*. With its rich visual
programme (a series of six images were created specifically for
this text) and pro-feminine message that modern audiences
have come to expect of Christine, it encapsulates several of the
elements that make up the enduring appeal of Christine's works.
Poetry, prose, letters, morality, pro-feminism, a spin on a common
narrative theme and a rich visual programme – more than any
of her other works, *Le Duc des vrais amans* encapsulates the
virtuosity of Christine's literary skills and exemplifies the features that make her work so remarkable. As such, this text is
well placed to replace the *Cité des dames* in the heart of modern
readers, especially those who wish to delve beyond Christine's
pro-feminine views. In any case, almost seven centuries after
her death, that Christine features on such an illustrious curric-
ulum as the *agrégation* confirms that she has found her place in
the French literary canon.

Artistic Encounters

Although there is no denying the popularity of Christine's works
from the middle of the twentieth century onwards, her main
impact on modern culture has been through the medium of visual
art rather than literature.

In recent years, there has been an explosion of artistic hom-
ages to Christine created by professional artists and amateur
fans alike, in online and physical spaces. One easy measure of
this is through social media: the hashtag #ChristinedePizan currently returns over 1,600 results on Instagram and the figure is
constantly rising. The tagged images are most often either artistic
recreations of illuminations of Christine's works, depictions of

Christine herself (many of which are fancy dress or cosplay in nature), or inspirational quotes from her works. Fans have fashioned her name out of crocheted granny squares and attached them to railings outside the Paris metro; they have reproduced and framed illuminations from her works, sewn her words in samplers that are displayed in embroidery hoops, and attributed the lines of her famous ballade 'Seulette sui' (Alone am I) to each of the star signs.[31] This interest is hardly surprising: Christine 'offers a well-documented name, a captivating life story, a large corpus of work, and compelling visual images, all of which combine to make her attractive and easy to use as an exemplar of medieval women'.[32] Visual aspects of her works also mean that she has been easily absorbed into social media.

In the hands of professional artists, tributes to Christine have become larger than life, one example being the nine-storey mural on the side of a building in Turin, created by the artist Camilla Falsini in 2018. The mural was created as part of the city's project 'Toward 2030', which aims to promote the global goals of the United Nations through street art. Falsini's contribution was commissioned to illustrate the particular goal of gender equality. The bold and fluorescent colours of Falsini's geometric representation depict Christine standing on top of a fortified building – a sign that it too was inspired by the *Cité des dames*. Its seven colours – three different shades of red or pink, as well as blue, black, white and fluorescent yellow – reflect the use of colour in the transgender and pansexual flags. In one hand, the five-storey-tall Christine holds up an open book, where the symbols for the male and female sexes are presented with an equal sign between them. A trail of ink stems from the female sign, connected to a pen in Christine's other hand.

Although it fits the gender-equality brief in a visually striking way, for viewers who are familiar with Christine's texts, the implication that she sought equality between the sexes will seem

Modern mural depicting the medieval author. Camilla Falsini,
Christine de Pizan, 2018.

inaccurate. Certainly, some of her writings anticipate the arguments made by modern feminists and her argument to respect women may seem close enough to the modern struggle for gender equality to be absorbed into that movement. But to suggest that she advocated equality between the sexes seems to diminish her efforts in calling for progress on issues that were more pressing at the time she was writing. Although these issues are all related, there is an implication that the goals of women from history need to be manipulated to match our current ones in order to be worthy of celebration. Works such as Falsini's contribute towards bringing Christine's name into the mainstream, but in revising her arguments and exchanging them for concerns that are in keeping with those of present-day audiences, she glosses over Christine's true views. Rather than being surprised to find that a medieval writer advocated for issues such as the education of girls and of women in business, modern readers are often disappointed not to find the medieval champion for female equality they have come to expect.

Despite these controversies, Falsini's is one of many artworks produced in the last sixty years in which Christine's legacy lives on. Across a range of artforms, several works celebrate her defences of women and her female creative force in radically different mediums.

Judy Chicago's 'The Dinner Party'

A key twentieth-century feminist artwork is Judy Chicago's 1979 installation *The Dinner Party*, a work that celebrates the contributions made by many women to global history. As its name suggests, it is, on a basic level, a table set for a dinner party at which places are laid for several notable women. It is in fact three tables – each measuring a little over 14 metres (46 ft) in length by 0.7 metres (26 in.) – laid out to form a triangle with places set for thirteen women along each of its sides. The women derive from three historical periods: from prehistory to Rome, Christianity to the Reformation and the American Revolution to the Women's Revolution. Christine's place is set on the second side of the triangle.[33]

But there is much more to *The Dinner Party* than a table. Each woman's place is decorated with an embroidered runner, set with a chalice, eating utensils and a china-painted porcelain plate. The decoration on the table runners and the motifs on the plates are designed to visually express something about each woman and the period in which she lived: the needlework on the runners makes use of techniques that were common to their individual lifetimes and the plates are decorated with vulvar and butterfly forms – symbols Chicago associated with women and liberation. The techniques used to create these details, embroidery and china painting, have traditionally been the preserve of women. Part of Chicago's goal in creating this installation was to commemorate and promote the various forms that woman's art has taken over the centuries, which have often been undervalued. The Christine de Pizan setting is embroidered using the bargello technique, a form of needlepoint that points to the author's Italian origins. The bargello creates sharp and 'angry . . . patterns [that] begin to encroach ever more severely on the space which surrounds the plate'.[34] Chicago explains that 'the sharp points are meant to indicate the increasingly difficult circumstances faced by women' at the end of the Middle Ages, but they also stand for the defamation of women against which Christine fought.[35] This aspect of her writings is represented in the plate, on which 'one wing of the butterfly form is raised in a gesture of defence, an image intended to symbolize her efforts to defend women through her writings.'[36]

There is more still to the installation: the three tables and their 39 settings sit on a 'Heritage Floor' made up of 2,300 tiles onto which the names of a further 999 women have been painted. 'This would suggest that the women at the table had risen from a foundation provided by other women's accomplishments,' Chicago explains.[37] Among the women associated with Christine are two medieval illuminators, one of whom is the artist Anastaise (briefly discussed in Chapter Two); Jane Anger – the sixteenth-century author of another proto-feminist text; Margaret Beaufort – the mother of Henry Tudor – celebrated for her erudition and contributions towards learning; Margery Kempe – a contemporary of Christine's and author of the first autobiography in the English language; and Margaret Paston, a fifteenth-century woman whose letters detailing her supervision of her husband's estates survive in *The Paston Letters*. Had she known of their existence, these are women whom Christine might even have thought to include in her own *Cité des dames*. In fact, Sappho, Judith – the biblical figure credited with having saved Israel – and the legendary female army of the Amazons, all of whom feature in Christine's text, also take their seat at Chicago's table, as do several of the other women on the Heritage Floor. As such, Chicago's installation is a kind of updated *Cité des dames*, with the difference that it is rendered in a visual, as opposed to primarily literary, medium.

Although Christine and Chicago both celebrate women's achievements by presenting a multitude of women in their respective mediums, there are some significant differences in their works. For one, Christine's aim of defending women, in which the fortifications of the city form a symbolic protective shield around them, is not present in Chicago's work, whose focus is on celebrating the contributions women have made to history and art. Another difference lies in the diversity of characters in Chicago's installation. Whereas Christine's scope was firmly on France and Italy and largely inspired by biblical sources and classical mythology, Chicago's vision is much more global,

Judy Chicago, *The Dinner Party* (Christine de Pizan place setting), 1974–9, mixed media (ceramic, porcelain, textile).

incorporating women from places as diverse as Mesopotamia, India, Assyria, the Americas and Oceania. Created several centuries after Christine, it is only natural that *The Dinner Party* would include a range of characters drawn from periods she had not yet known, but it also stretches back further into our prehistory than the *Cité* does, to include female abstractions such as the Primordial Goddess and the Fertile Goddess. In spite of these differences, Christine's and Chicago's creations share the same goal of recording the contributions women have made in history and inscribing them in art.

The connection between Christine's text and Chicago's installation and the similarities between the two works has in turn been explored in a series of 27 collages created by the artist Marsha Pippenger, *Dinner in the City* (2007). Like *La Cité des dames* and *The Dinner Party*, Pippenger's exhibit is tripartite in structure. It begins with a series of collages that depict the main events from the opening of *La Cité des dames*, including Christine reading misogynous works and falling into a dream, the appearance of the three virtuous ladies and the building of the City itself.[38] In this series, Pippenger has incorporated details from Christine's manuscripts into her collages, depicting Christine in a similar costume to the one she wears in the illuminations prepared by the City of Ladies Master and using a similar chequerboard pattern for the background (see examples in the Introduction and Chapter Two). The second series treats *The Dinner Party* in a similar way, featuring portraits of some of the ladies featured in Chicago's installation. Once again, Pippenger reproduces details from the place settings at Chicago's table in her own representations.

The final series of collages imagines the meeting of Judy Chicago and Christine de Pizan, showing them 'begin to infiltrate each other's collages as their stories come together'.[39] In the first image, Christine is sat at her desk reading as a beam of light comes through the window – echoing the beam of light that announces the arrival of the three virtuous ladies in the *Cité*. Behind her, Chicago's figure emerges from the background – appearing almost as a shadow. The next images in this series describe the meeting of Chicago and Christine as they touch hands; later, Christine sits in her place at *The Dinner Party*, the architectural City of Ladies represented through a window in the distance. This third series culminates in a collage entitled 'Looking Forward' – an explosive piece showing 'the past, present, and future of women and their achievements' that

Marsha Pippenger, 'All of a Sudden, I Saw a Beam of Light', 2007, paper on canvas. Christine, observed by Judy Chicago, is inspired to start writing.

Marsha Pippenger, 'Looking Forward', 2007, paper on canvas. Christine,
Judy Chicago and the future woman come together.

includes three women: Christine stands for the past, Chicago 'for the struggles of contemporary women', and the third, faceless figure represents women who are yet to come. The bright, flame-like points around the collage border replicate the colours and shapes of the bargello work in Chicago's installation, while the chequerboard pattern once again recalls the background of illu-minations in Christine's manuscripts. *The Dinner Party* and the *Cité des dames* are visually merged. In juxtaposing different female artistic mediums of needlepoint, collage and women's writing, this image renders various facets of female cultural, literary and artistic heritage. The six hundred years separating Christine, Chicago and Pippenger are annihilated in a celebratory image that encompasses all women.

Twenty-first-century Artistic Reimaginings of the 'Cité des dames'

Christine's architectural City of Ladies might only appear in the background of Pippenger's collages, but it takes centre stage in the designs of two twenty-first-century artists, one of which is a work by Tai Shani that went on to win the Turner Prize in 2019. This large-scale installation, entitled DC: *Semiramis*, is an artis-tic and psychedelic expansion of Christine's *Cité* that encompasses live performative and sculptural features. On its most funda-mental level, the installation itself is a site on which the idea of a City of Ladies is imagined through sculptural elements. It has an unsettling, otherworldly feel to it: on the floor, the outlines of various structures rise in shallow reliefs while severed pillars and other, organic shapes float overhead. An enormous green hand, made from card, foam and a resinous material called Jesmonite, lies palm-up on the floor. Several smaller pairs of hands holding small geometrical shapes lie in a line across the front of the set. It is unclear whether this is physically a City of Ladies or (per-haps more realistically) intended as a starting point from which

the viewer can imagine what such a city might be like. Shani
herself says her installation is not a physical city, as it is supposed to exist in time and not space, and neither is it a place
for women alone but for a more inclusive femininity in general.
'It's . . . a city that is for anyone that wants to live outside a white
supremacist, capitalist patriarchy,' she explains.⁴⁰

The installation is populated by twelve characters, invented
by Shani, each of whom delivers a monologue. Shani's creations
are drawn from history and myth (like Christine's) but also
science-fiction narratives and software. Characters include The
Woman on the Edge of Time, The Medieval Mystic, Phantasma-
goregasm and the intriguingly named Psy Chic Anem One.⁴¹
During live performances, their monologues play on a separate
screen while the bodies of thirteen women move about the
installation. Like the names of the women in the videos, the
costumes of those occupying the installation reflect their origins
in different historical periods: one wears a long, flowing white
Grecian gown, one a medieval-style bottle-green velvet robe,
another a fluffy orange leotard. Several of them are near-nude,
wearing only light skin-coloured shorts, accessorized for some of
the performers with elbow-length gloves or a brightly coloured
cape. The installation and performance are presented within an
immersive and sensual space in which the colours of the walls
and the music envelop the viewer, allowing them also to tem-
porarily escape reality and take up residence in the city.

Shani's work is only a loose adaptation of Christine's text,
but it does share several aspects with its medieval antecedent.
In addition to taking inspiration from history and mythology,
both artists have created a utopia (literally a non-place) in their
respective works: while Shani's explicitly says that hers exists
outside of space, Christine's is engendered in a dream vision.
For both creators, the spaces they have designed are places of
refuge from a state of affairs that does not favour women. Both

cities are also populated, although Shani's characters are more imaginary 'types' around whom narratives have been composed, as opposed to the historical beings whose familiar stories ground the reader in the *Cité*. The name of Shani's installation, *Semiramis*, is itself drawn directly from a chapter in Christine's text, where Semiramis is celebrated as a warrior and conqueror who 'founded and rebuilt a number of cities and fortifications' in Africa and India. Christine also mentions 'a large statue in the form of a richly gilded, copper figure on a tall pillar in Babylon' that commemorated her quashing a revolt.[42] Could it be that the large green hand that takes centre stage in the installation represents the disembodied hand of this copper statue? If so, this indicates that the City of Ladies Shani imagines is not modelled on ancient, fortified cities – even one built by a woman – but is formed from the rubble of past works of literature.

These two projects both also draw on their creators' personal experience. *La Cité des dames* is a response to the fact that Christine saw so much misogyny in the writings of her predecessors and contemporaries. There is more than a hint of the autobiographical in the opening of this text, especially in Christine's lamentation over the depiction of women and perhaps even extending to her outburst that she wishes she had been born a man. Similarly, the various women whose stories make up the book and whose bodies enter the city are women drawn from Christine's own experiences, even if she has only encountered them through reading. From that point of view, Christine's city is a monument to her personal experience and to the literary grounding she has cultivated in the 'field of letters' – the place that Lady Reason chooses to build the city.[43] Shani also hints at the role her own personal experience played in conceiving the various components of *Semiramis*. Like Christine, she outlines its influence in terms of a building metaphor, describing it as an 'excavation' into 'personal and shared gender trauma that I've experienced'.[44] For both, there is a conscious effort to use the personal narratives of women to give shape to artistic and literary creation, a move that valorizes female experiences in the process.

Penelope Haralambidou of the Bartlett School of Architecture is another artist to have created an installation based on the *Cité des dames*, though hers takes much more immediate inspiration from Christine's work and its illuminations. Her *City of Ladies* exhibit, which was on show at London's Domobaal gallery early in 2020, comprises an installation and a film.[45] Haralambidou describes her work as an allegory, presenting a reading of the text and its illuminations from an architectural point of view. It began as a project on writing surfaces and vellum: she was interested in the fact that with the advent of digital design, the drawing space has effectively been lost and only appears when works are printed. This led her to examine how architecture was used in medieval manuscripts and from there to the architectural model presented in Christine's *Cité des dames*. This initial interest in the interaction of flat drawing spaces and three-dimensional architecture is seen in three of the installation's focal objects: these are 3D models of the architectural spaces seen in the 'Queen's Manuscript' version of the *Cité des dames*.

The 3D models sit on three tables that are covered with sheets of parchment, each table corresponding to one of the three parts of Christine's text. Details have been drawn on the vellum surface using gilding of gold, silver and white gold leaf with rounded glass paperweights dotted around to highlight certain features. Some of them – such as a map of Paris with the location of the Louvre highlighted in gold and an architectural plan of the tower containing the library – draw out connections between Christine and her historical setting in medieval Paris. Other details respond directly to her miniatures: one is a floor plan of one of the illuminations of the *Cité des dames* that can be seen in Chapter Two, showing the study on one side and the city under construction on the other, connected by a kind of tube. The walls of the city have been drawn thicker, their hard brick structure rendered soft and supple through a series of lines and globules of gold and silver ink – details that conjure biological diagrams of the fleshy walls of a placenta.

The idea of conception is merely hinted at in the diagram but is expanded into a full metaphor in a video that plays on a loop next to the installation. It begins by representing the 3D model of the room depicted in the left-hand panel of the same illumination, the room in which Christine is shown in discussion with the three virtuous ladies. A fleshy white globule launches out of this room into an empty space where the right-hand panel of the illumination shows the foundations of the city being built, though it remains connected to the desk by a kind of cord. Soon, the desk is pulled out of the room by the cord and the architectural structure that had contained it fades away. In its place, the city depicted in the other miniatures slowly begins to take shape, starting as an indistinct, almost melted, shape but gradually expanding and forming into distinct structures and buildings. As one of the other two 3D models slowly takes shape from the melted material, the corresponding illumination is projected onto its cityscape. Sounds have been added to the video – the pulse of a heart, liquids oozing and bubbling, the muffled sound of a female voice. These confirm that what is being shown is the city growing inside a womb.

Metaphorically, the architectural city (shown in the right-hand panel of the illumination) has become a placenta that allows the foetus to which it is attached (Christine's book, represented by the desk that was extracted from the study) to grow. Following the metaphor through might lead us to wonder what the city-placenta is meant to filter out. The answer is of course misogyny. The absorbent walls protect the book-foetus from all forms of

Penelope Haralambidou, *City of Ladies*, 2020, installation at
Domobaal, London.

anti-feminine thought and allow it to grow. In Christine's text,
the relationship between the book and the city was a metaphorical one, in which the city formed a metaphorical double for
the book (as seen in Chapter Three), but the opening miniature of the work has lent itself surprisingly well to the conception
metaphor, only requiring a little manipulation to take on this
additional layer of meaning. In this visual medium, the City of
Ladies arguably takes on greater dimensions than it could in the
text.

Like Shani's adaptation, Haralambidou's also has a utopian,
feminist strand that probes at the architectural theme of the
Cité. 'If we had to start from scratch and build a City of Ladies,
from where would we start, and how would it be different?', she
asks. To explore this question, Haralambidou took the three
objects that the virtuous ladies carry in Christine's narrative
(a mirror, a ruler and a vessel) as a focus for her exhibit and

reimagined them in a feminine way. So, for instance, the mirror is not flat, but curved and malleable, suggesting a different way of looking at things; the markings on the ruler are moulded around Haralambidou's fingers, allowing measurements to be made using female dimensions. The final object is a vessel, cast as an hourglass, intended to measure time. Its purpose is to signal that a city conceived around female dimensions has not yet been made possible and to ask when such a city might be built. The means of constructing the glass vessel echo the biological formation of the architectural models in the video: it too started as a ball of liquid glass that gradually expanded and was crafted into its finished form.

Although Christine's idea of a City of Ladies – a city that prioritizes female history, dimensions, needs and stories – has seized the imagination of artists like Shani and Haralambidou, what both of their installations reveal are the difficulties of conceptualizing such a city in reality. While Shani's city is intended to exist only in the abstract, Haralambidou's poses more questions than it answers. How will it be made? What will it look like? When will it be built, and where? The fact that these questions are still being asked six hundred years after Christine first imagined her own City of Ladies could seem to rather pessimistically suggest that little progress has been made. However, each of these adaptations has also expanded and advanced Christine's initial concept in significant ways. Shani and Chicago have together increased the original population of the *Cité*; Chicago and Pippenger have added a dimension that celebrates women's material culture. Shani and Haralambidou take Christine's abstract concept and begin to pose practical questions about how and where a city might be built. In their own ways, each of these works demonstrates the potential for literature and the visual arts to create spaces that are more accessible to women. But undoubtedly where they are most optimistic is as a collective, in showing that there is no one City of Ladies. Of all the ways in which Christine's *Cité* has been reimagined by modern artists, only Chicago's succeeds in creating a physical space. Yet that the tradition of imagining a City of Ladies is six hundred years old demonstrates the timelessness of the concept: such a city certainly exists in time, if not in physical space.

A Different Christine de Pizan for Every Generation

Over the course of the last six centuries, Christine de Pizan's legacy has taken the form of multiple afterlives across successive generations. She was celebrated by the poets who immediately followed her, only to be largely cast out of the literary canon in the early modern period and then welcomed back into it in the twentieth century. Each generation has maintained a particular fascination with her on the grounds of her sex while also recasting their own version of 'Christine de Pizan'. In the early modern period, she was celebrated as a poet, while she was thought of as a historian at the start of the modern era. Today, much of the fascination she has earned is due to her reputation as a feminist writer. Although the modern fascination with her pro-feminine works (in particular *La Cité des dames*) has granted Christine a large following, this interest can be criticized for being somewhat narrow in focus. In some cases, it has resulted in appropriations that ascribe to Christine views that she simply did not have.

As anachronistic as some of these ideas might be, feminist interest in Christine has opened her works to a wider audience than she could have ever imagined. Entering the mainstream has had the effect of shifting the perception of women in the Middle Ages in general, since her example alone serves to debunk the idea that medieval women were all unhappily married, illiterate and excluded from political matters. Few medieval writers have infiltrated the popular imagination of successive generations in the way that Christine has done, nor can many claim to have had such an impact on the cultural landscape of the future. For the time being at least, the legacy of this medieval author seems set to endure.

Conclusion

Have regard to thy name; for that shall continue.
Le Livre des trois vertus[1]

C hristine de Pizan was a writer who engaged so actively
with her heritage and participated in so many different
aspects of her wider contemporary culture that it is
almost impossible to consider her outside of any cultural context. Cultural considerations shaped every aspect of her works,
from the making and manufacture of her books which she oversaw so carefully, to the popular themes and fashionable poetic
forms in and about which she wrote, to the contemporary political issues with which she engaged so forthrightly. They even
affected the very course of her life, since it was the cultural
climate of medieval Paris that brought her family to the city in
the first place and later allowed her to make a living. It is therefore only fitting that Christine's legacy has been to have an
enduring impact on modern-day culture. Her life, works and
legacy are from that perspective quite unique.

When the National Women's History Museum in Virginia
set up their Women Making History Awards, the gala event was
named after Christine. This award ceremony celebrates the
contributions of women to the modern cultural landscape for
their vision, determination and perseverance – characteristics
they share with the medieval author. In November 2011 the

inaugural Christine de Pizan Honors Gala was presided over by the multiple-award-winning actress Meryl Streep. It was followed by a second gala in 2012 that also bore Christine's name at which women from across the cultural spectrum were presented with Living Legacy awards. They included the acclaimed photographer Annie Leibovitz, the prolific poet, essayist and civil rights activist Maya Angelou, and the former U.S. Senator Elizabeth Dole. Politically and culturally engaged women from the fields of art, writing and politics: an appropriate set of women to celebrate at an event in Christine's name and a further testament to her enduring legacy.

What will future generations find of interest in Christine's works? Will they come to ignore the writer and instead focus entirely on the make-up of her books – breaking down the individual quires she so carefully compiled to understand how they were produced, scanning each page under UV light to uncover the secrets of their manufacture? Will the innovations she brought to her writing be played down as she comes to be viewed as a plagiarist who copied her sources? It seems her legacy as a defender of women has been secured, but as the waves of feminism continue to ebb and flow, those who have praised her pro-feminine efforts might turn against her – as some already have – to denounce her conservative, radical form of proto-feminism.

It should come as no surprise that Christine has already been commercialized – her face appearing on T-shirts, tote bags, mugs and cushions alongside quotations that sometimes do (but often do not) come directly from her works. A silver pendant depicting her in discussion with the Sibyl in *Le Livre du chemin de long estude* (The Book of the Path of Long Study) is one of several Christine-inspired pieces of jewellery available for purchase on websites such as Etsy and Ruby Lane. Some of her lyric poetry has been set to music and can be listened to in recordings by the likes of the VocaMe ensemble. She has inspired some writers of fiction, too, appearing as a character in several recent novels, including a series by Tania Bayard in which she plays a Sherlock Holmes-type solver of mysteries. It seems only a matter of time before she makes her first on-screen appearance as a film or television character.

It would be easy to dismiss all of this as commercialism, the monetization of a historical figure that profits a few individuals. But a less cynical view is that these examples show that Christine has become a recognizable enough figure for such products to exist. She is not quite so mainstream as to be a household name in the way that Geoffrey Chaucer is in England, but she is distinct enough to be remembered as a unique medieval persona. The range of the products on which she features and the incarnations that Christine currently occupies testify that she has been absorbed into twenty-first-century culture.

One might assume that a woman who has been dead for almost six hundred years can only stay relevant for so long, but if anything, the surge of popular interest in Christine feels like it is just getting started. It was only in 2016 that a new road in the seventeenth arrondissement of Paris was named after her. Although it is rather regrettable that its name uses the archaic form of her name, Pisan (a spelling used when her family were believed to have originated from the town of Pisa, when they actually hailed from Pizzano), this is still a sign of Christine's cultural significance having recently been recognized. After all, streets are usually named to acknowledge the lasting legacy of an individual, not in order to bring someone into mainstream consciousness.

Gala-award ceremonies, artwork, jewellery, books and music: Christine has amassed quite a cultural capital. The historical Christine de Pizan may have died around 1431 but there is no denying that, in a number of different guises, she is very much alive today. The direction of interest in Christine has always been driven by publications deriving from academic research. It is from here that the interest in Christine's pro-feminine stance proceeded from the nineteenth century onwards. But, in recent decades, this strand of Christine studies has begun to fall out of fashion and research into her works has taken a wider range of their characteristics into consideration. The political views they display are being probed, as are visual aspects of her manuscripts. After a hiatus of several centuries, the form and versification of Christine's lyric poetry are also once again under scrutiny. In future years, these elements of her works might too come to filter into popular culture just as her pro-feminine ideas have recently made their way out of the ivory tower and into our art galleries, and even onto our streets.

CHRONOLOGY

1398	Christine's son Jean enters the household of the Earl of Salisbury in England
c. 1399	Christine produces her first manuscripts
c. 1400	Jean de Montreuil writes treatise in praise of *Le Roman de la rose*
1401	Philip of Burgundy and Louis of Orleans by now opposed on all contemporary political issues. Christine writes to Montreuil, triggering the start of the debate of the *Romance of the Rose*
1403	Christine presents the first significant collection of her works to the Queen of France
1404	Death of Philip, Duke of Burgundy; title passes to his son, John
1405	August: John of Burgundy marches on Paris with eight hundred men bearing concealed arms. October: peace treaty signed between the Dukes of Burgundy and Orleans
1407	20 November: John of Burgundy and Louis of Orleans undertake oath of ritual brotherhood to put aside enmity. 23 November: John of Burgundy murders Louis of Orleans in Paris; title of Duke of Orleans passes to Louis' son, Charles
c. 1408	Christine begins work on 'The Queen's Manuscript'
1410	Christine urges John of Berry and Isabeau of Bavaria to help de-escalate tension between Burgundians and Orleanists
1411	Louis of Orleans' sons at war against John of Burgundy
1413	Cabochian Revolt, backed by John of Burgundy, fails; the duke flees Paris
1415	Led by Henry v, the English inflict a crushing defeat on the French at Agincourt
1417	The Bastille begins to serve as a prison
1418	May–August: massacre of Orleanists and Armagnacs in Paris at hands of the Burgundians. Many nobles flee the city, among them Christine and Isabeau
1419	John of Burgundy assassinated by the dauphin's men in October
1420	English and French sign the Treaty of Troyes in May, recognizing Henry v of England as heir and regent to the French throne
1422	Death of Henry v of England in August, followed by that of Charles vi of France in October. John, Duke of Bedford, governs Paris during the future Henry vi's minority

1429	Joan of Arc leads the French to victory at Orleans
	Christine pens her final work, *Le Ditié Jehanne d'Arc*,
	in Joan's honour. Charles VII of France crowned at Reims
	cathedral
1430	Joan captured by the Burgundians, who hand her over
	to the English; she is tried by Burgundian and English
	clerics and executed in Rouen the following year
c. 1431	Death of Christine de Pizan
c. 1450	Gutenberg's printing press in operation
1453	End of Hundred Years War

REFERENCES

Introduction

1 Christine de Pizan, *The Book of the Path of Long Study*, in *The Selected Writings of Christine de Pizan*, ed. Renate Blumenfeld-Kosinski, trans. Renate Blumenfeld-Kosinski and Kevin Brownlee (New York and London, 1997), p. 75.

2 Charity Cannon Willard, *Christine de Pizan: Her Life and Works* (New York, 1982), p. 17.

3 Christine de Pizan, *Othea's Letter to Hector*, ed. and trans. Renate Blumenfeld-Kosinski and Earl Jeffrey Richards (Toronto, 2017), p. 32.

4 Christine de Pizan, *The Book of the City of Ladies and Other Writings*, ed. Sophie Bourgault and Rebecca Kingston, trans. Ineke Hardy (Indianapolis, IN, and Cambridge, 2018), p. 141.

5 Christine de Pizan, *Christine's Vision*, ed. and trans. Glenda McLeod (London, 1993), p. 110.

6 Christine de Pizan, *The Book of Fortune's Transformation*, in *Selected Writings*, pp. 101–2.

7 Christine de Pizan, *Christine's Vision*, p. 111.

8 Simone Roux, *Christine de Pizan: Femme de tête, dame de cœur* (Paris, 2006).

9 Willard, *Life and Works*, pp. 39–40.

10 Christine de Pizan, *Fortune's Transformation*, p. 106.

11 Jeff Rider, 'Becoming a Man: Christine de Pizan, 1390 to 1400', in *Approaches to Teaching the Works of Christine de Pizan*, ed. Andrea Tarnowski (New York, 2018), pp. 34–41 (p. 37).

12 See Patrick M. de Winter, 'Christine de Pizan, ses enlumineurs et ses rapports avec le milieu bourguignon', in *Actes du 104ᵉ congrès national des sociétés savantes. Section de philologie et d'histoire jusqu'à 1610. Bordeaux, 1979* (Paris, 1981), pp. 335–75.

13 Deborah McGrady, *The Writer's Gift or the Patron's Pleasure?: The Literary Economy in Late Medieval France* (Toronto, 2019), pp. 44–52, gives a fascinating insight into medieval networks of patronage and gift-giving.

14 In this ballade, Christine describes herself as having grieved
   for five years, which (assuming her grief is connected to her
   husband's death) would mean the poem was composed in 1395.
   It is reproduced in *Œuvres poétiques de Christine de Pizan*,
   ed. Maurice Roy (Paris, 1886), vol. i, p. 10.
15 See Jane Taylor, *The Making of Poetry: Late Medieval French
   Poetic Anthologies* (Turnhout, 2007), pp. 13–20.
16 Ibid.
17 Christine de Pizan, *Rondeaux*, in *Œuvres poétiques*, vol. i,
   p. 148. My translation.
18 Christine de Pizan, *Cent balades*, in *Œuvres* poétiques, vol. i,
   p. 12. My translation.
19 Christine de Pizan, *Christine's Vision*, p. 122.
20 As Karen Green demonstrated in her recent article 'Was
   Christine de Pizan at Poissy 1418–1429?', *Medium Aevum*,
   LXIII/1 (2014), pp. 28–40, this cannot have been the case.
21 Christine de Pizan, *The Tale of Joan of Arc*, in *Selected Writings*,
   pp. 253–62.
22 Ibid., p. 257.

1 A Visit to Christine de Pizan's Paris

1 Christine de Pizan, *Christine's Vision*, ed. and trans. Glenda
   McLeod (London, 1993), p. 14.
2 On medieval Paris, see Philippe Lorentz and Dany Sandron's
   *Atlas de Paris au Moyen Âge: Espace urbain, habitat, société,
   religion, lieux de pouvoir* (Paris, 2006); Boris Bove and Claude
   Girard, eds, *Le Paris du Moyen Âge* (Paris, 2018); and the
   website 'Atlas Historique de Paris', http://paris-atlas-
   historique.fr.
3 Bove and Girard, eds, *Paris du Moyen Âge*, p. 29.
4 Ibid., p. 20.
5 Henrietta Leyser, *Medieval Women: A Social History
   of Women in England, 450–1500* (London, 1995),
   p. 159.
6 Quotations from *Le Livre des trois vertus* are taken from
   the translation in *The Selected Writings of Christine
   de Pizan*, ed. Renate Blumenfeld-Kosinski, trans. Renate
   Blumenfeld-Kosinski and Kevin Brownlee (New York
   and London, 1997).
7 Ibid.

8 Christine de Pizan, *Le Livre des fais et bonnes meurs du sage roy Charles v*, ed. Susan Solente (Paris, 1936–40), vol. II, p. 37. Translations of this text are my own.

9 Further information on medieval Paris and the city walls can be found on the 'Atlas Historique de Paris' website, see http://paris-atlas-historique.fr, accessed 3 July 2021.

10 The Bastille is remembered largely as a prison, though it was not built to serve this purpose; nor was it used to hold prisoners until 1417.

11 In her biography of Christine de Pizan, *Christine de Pisan, 1364–1430: Étude biographique et littéraire* (Paris, 1927), Marie-Josèphe Pinet cites archival documents showing that, before his death, Charles v made a gift of the Tour Barbeau to Etienne.

12 Christine de Pizan, *Fais et bonnes meurs*, vol. 1 (1936), p. 142.

13 Deborah McGrady, *The Writer's Gift or the Patron's Pleasure? The Literary Economy in Late Medieval France* (Toronto, 2019), p. 31.

14 Françoise Autrand, *Charles v: Le Sage* (Paris, 1994).

15 Yann Potin, 'À la recherche de la librairie du Louvre', *Gazette du livre médiéval*, XXXIV (1999), pp. 25–36 (p. 34).

16 McGrady, *Writer's Gift*, p. 39.

17 'History of the Bodleian', www.bodleian.ox.ac.uk, accessed 8 March 2021.

18 Viscount Dillon, 'Inventory of the Goods . . . Belonging to Thomas, Duke of Gloucester', *Archaeological Journal*, LIV (1897), pp. 275–308 (p. 281).

19 Florence Bouchet, *Le Discours sur la lecture en France aux XIVe et XVe siècles: Pratiques, poétique, imaginaire* (Paris, 2008), pp. 12–13.

20 'The Vernon Manuscript: A Literary Hoard from Medieval England', www.bodleian.ox.ac.uk, accessed 8 March 2021.

21 Michelle P. Brown, ed., *The Luttrell Psalter* (London, 2006) p. 6.

22 Pierre Champion, *La Librairie de Louis d'Orléans* (Paris, 1910), p. xvi.

23 McGrady, *Writer's Gift*, pp. 31–2.

24 Ibid., p. 47.

25 Ibid., p. 42.

26 Tracy Adams's book *Christine de Pizan and the Fight for France* (University Park, PA, 2014), describes the events in detail and admirably highlights the political context of many of Christine's texts.

27 Christine de Pizan, *Christine's Vision*, p. 27.

28 See Adams, *Fight*, pp. 154–60.

29 *'The Epistle of the Prison of Human Life'* with *'An Epistle to the Queen of France'* and *'Lament on the Evils of the Civil War'*, ed. and trans. Josette Wisman (New York, 1984), p. 89.

30 This is the central argument of Adams, *Fight*.

31 Adams, *Fight*, pp. 107–12.

32 Sandra Hindman, *Christine de Pizan's 'Epistre Othea': Painting and Politics at the Court of Charles VI* (Wetteren, 1986), pp. 34–51.

33 Christine de Pizan, *Othea's Letter to Hector*, ed. and trans. Renate Blumenfeld-Kosinski and Earl Jeffrey Richards (Toronto, 2017), p. 34.

34 P.G.C. Campbell, 'Christine de Pisan en Angleterre', *Revue de littérature comparée*, V (1925), pp. 659–70.

2 Christine's Artistic Vision

1 Christine de Pizan, *The Book of the City of Ladies and Other Writings*, ed. Sophie Bourgault and Rebecca Kingston, trans. Ineke Hardy (Indianapolis, IN, and Cambridge, 2018), pp. 86–7.

2 Louisa Dunlop, 'Pigments and Painting Materials in Fourteenth- and Early Fifteenth-century Parisian Manuscript Illumination', in *Artistes, artisans et production artistique au Moyen Age, Colloque international, Centre national de la recherche scientifique, Université de Rennes II-Haute Bretagne, 2–6 Mai 1983*, ed. Xavier Barral i Altet (Paris, 1990), vol. III, pp. 271–93. Also see Spike Bucklow, *The Alchemy of Paint: Art, Science and Secrets from the Middle Ages* (London, 2009).

3 The manuscripts in question are Paris, Bibliothèque nationale de France, MSS fr. 1643 and 604.

4 Mary Rouse and Richard Rouse, 'La Famille d'André le Musnier, de 1400 jusqu'à 1511', in *Pratiques de la culture écrite en France au XVᵉ siècle*, ed. N. Pons and M. Ornato (Louvain-la-Neuve, 1995), pp. 379–87.

5 Kouky Fianu, 'Métiers et espace: Topographie de la fabrication et du commerce du livre à Paris (XIIIᵉ–XVᵉ siècles)', in *Patrons, Authors and Workshops: Books and Book Production in Paris around 1400*, ed. Godfried Croenen and Peter F. Ainsworth (Louvain, 2006), pp. 21–45.

6 Gilbert Ouy et al. attribute only this image to the Bedford Master in the *Album Christine de Pizan* (Turnhout, 2012). However, in *French Painting in the Time of Jean de Berry: The Late Fourteenth Century and the Patronage of the Duke* (London, 1967), Millard

Meiss attributed five of the manuscript's miniatures to a Master of the Bedford Trend. 'The Queen's Manuscript' can be viewed online in its entirety at 'Digitised Manuscripts', 'Harley MS 4431' (the image is on fol. 56v), www.bl.uk, accessed 8 March 2021.

7 Musée du Louvre, *Paris 1400: Les Arts sous Charles VI* (Paris, 2004), p. 137.

8 Sandra Hindman, 'The Composition of the Manuscript of Christine de Pizan's Collected Works in the British Library: A Reassessment', *British Library Journal*, IX (1983), pp. 93–123.

9 James Laidlaw, 'Christine de Pizan: The Making of the Queen's Manuscript (London, British Library, Harley 4431)', in *Patrons, Authors and Workshops*, ed. Croenen and Ainsworth, pp. 297–310 (pp. 306–7).

10 Ibid.

11 Details of all of the manuscripts Christine produced can be found in Ouy et al., *Album*.

12 Christine de Pizan, *Christine's Vision*, ed. and trans. Glenda McLeod (London, 1993), p. 119.

13 Adapted from ibid., p. 120.

14 The first modern edition of Christine's works is a three-volume collection prepared by Maurice Roy between 1886 and 1896. Christine's handwriting was confirmed by Gilbert Ouy and Christine Reno in a study entitled 'Identification des autographes de Christine de Pizan', *Scriptorium*, XXXIV (1980), pp. 221–38. More than thirty years of subsequent research led to the *Album* being prepared by Ouy et al.

15 Olivier Delsaux, 'Profil d'un des copistes des manuscrits originaux de Christine de Pizan: P. De La Croix, alias la main R', *Scriptorium*, LXV (2011), pp. 251–97.

16 Ouy et al., *Album*, pp. 23–5.

17 Although their hands have not been identified with certainty, the English medieval authors John Gower and Thomas Hoccleve, the Italian writer Petrarch and the French author Guillaume de Machaut are believed to have exerted some authorial control over the copying of their texts, if not scribed them themselves.

18 Ouy et al., *Album*, p. 25. Translation mine.

19 Ouy and Reno, 'Identification'.

20 Ouy et al., *Album*, p. 37.

21 Olivier Delsaux, *Manuscrits et pratiques autographes chez les écrivains français de la fin du moyen âge: L'Exemple de Christine de Pizan* (Geneva, 2013), pp. 518–20.

22 In particular, the start of *L'Epistre Othea* and *Le Chemin de long estude* (on fols 95r and 178r respectively).

23 Tania Van Hemelryck and Christine Reno, 'Dans l'atelier de Christine de Pizan. Le Manuscrit Harley 4431', *Pecia*, XIII (January 2010), pp. 267–86.

24 Ibid.

25 I have slightly modified the passage from *The Book of the City of Ladies*, ed. Bourgault and Kingston, pp. 86–7, which anglicizes Anastaise to 'Anastasia'.

26 Inès Villela-Petit, 'À la recherche d'Anastaise', *Cahiers de recherches médiévales*, XVI (2008), pp. 301–16.

27 As suggested by Inès Villela-Petit in Ouy et al., *Album*, p. 104.

28 Ibid., pp. 154–68.

29 See Luke Syson, 'Introduction' to *The Image of the Individual: Portraits in the Renaissance*, ed. Nicholas Mann and Lyke Syson (London, 1998), pp. 9–14.

30 See Michel Pastoureau, *Blue: The History of a Color* (Princeton, NJ, and Oxford, 2001).

31 Michael T. Clanchy, *From Memory to Written Record: England, 1066–1307* (Oxford and Malden, 2013), p. 192.

32 Christine de Pizan, *City*, p. 27.

33 Jacqueline Cerquiglini-Toulet, *The Colour of Melancholy*, trans. Lydia G. Cochrane (Baltimore, MD, and London, 1997), p. 73.

34 Christine de Pizan, *City*, p. 23.

35 Christine de Pizan, *L'Oroyson Nostre Dame*, in *Œuvres poétiques de Christine de Pizan*, ed. Maurice Roy (Paris, 1896), vol. III, pp. 1–9 (p. 2). All translations of *L'Oroyson* are mine.

36 Christine de Pizan, *L'Oroyson*, p. 5.

37 Gordon Kipling, *Enter the King: Theatre, Liturgy, and Ritual in the Medieval Civic Triumph* (Oxford, 1998), p. 294.

38 Tracy Adams, *The Life and Afterlife of Isabeau of Bavaria* (Baltimore, MD, 2010), p. 110.

39 Ibid.

40 The full manuscript reference is Leiden, Bibliotheek der Rijksuniversteit, Ltk 1819.

41 Laidlaw, 'The Queen's Manuscript', p. 297.

42 See Charlotte E. Cooper, 'A Reassessment of Christine de Pizan's Didactic Works', unpublished DPhil thesis (University of Oxford, 2017).

3 Christine Stems the Fountain of Misogyny

1 Adapted from Christine de Pizan, *The Book of the City of Ladies and Other Writings*, ed. Sophie Bourgault and Rebecca Kingston, trans. Ineke Hardy (Cambridge, 2018), p. 22.

2 Christine de Pizan, *The Book of the Path of Long Study*, in *The Selected Writings of Christine de Pizan*, ed. Renate Blumenfeld-Kosinski, trans. Renate Blumenfeld-Kosinski and Kevin Brownlee (New York and London, 1997), p. 63. The original French text was written in verse.

3 Christine de Pizan, *The Book of Deeds of Arms and of Chivalry*, trans. Sumner Willard, ed. Charity Cannon Willard (University Park, PA, 1999), p. 144.

4 Ibid.

5 Christine de Pizan, *City*, p. 21.

6 Ibid., p. 22. The book that Christine reads is *Les Lamentations de Matheolus* (The Book of Matheolus' Lamentations), a text in which the protagonist laments all of the misfortune that has befallen him since he got married.

7 Adapted from ibid., p. 22. I have substituted 'endless fountain' for the translators' 'bubbling', to convey the constant renewal of the fountain suggested in the Old French *ressourdant*.

8 Ibid.

9 Ibid., p. 26.

10 Alfred Jeanroy, 'Boccace et Christine de Pisan: Le *De claris mulieribus*, principale source du *Livre de la cité des dames*', *Romania*, XLVIII (1922), pp. 93–105 (p. 94). Translation my own.

11 See Cynthia J. Brown, *Poets, Patrons and Printers: Crisis of Authority in Late Medieval France* (London, 1995), pp. 28–9.

12 Giovanni Boccaccio, *Famous Women*, ed. and trans. Virginia Brown (Cambridge, MA, 2001), pp. 10–11.

13 Ibid., p. 175.

14 Christine de Pizan, *City*, p. 34.

15 Although both might be translated as 'pleasure', in the *Rose*, this character is named Deduiz, whereas in Froissart's text, it is Plaisance.

16 See Jacqueline Cerquiglini-Toulet, '*Un engin si soutil*': *Guillaume de Machaut et l'écriture au XIVe siècle* (Geneva, 1985), pp. 77–8.

17 René of Anjou, *The Book of the Love-smitten Heart*, ed. and trans. Stephanie Viereck Gibbs and Kathryn Karczewska (London, 2001), p. 231.

18 Guillaume de Lorris and Jean de Meun, *The Romance of the Rose*,
   ed. and trans. Charles Dahlberg (Princeton, NJ, 1995), pp. 165–6.
   This prose translation does not pack a punch in quite the same way
   as the Old French verse:

   > Toutes estes, serez ou fustes
   > De fait ou de voulenté, pustes!
   > Car, qui que puist le fait estaindre,
   > Volenté ne puet nus contraindre.
   > Tel avantage ont toutes fames
   > qu'eus sunt de leur volentez dames:
   > L'en ne vous puet les cures changier
   > Pour batre ne pour laidangier.
   > Mais qui changier les vous peüst,
   > Des cors la seigneurie eüst.

   Le Roman de la rose, ed. Armand Strubel (Paris, 1992), ll. 9159–68.
19 *Romance of the Rose*, ed. and trans. Dahlberg, p. 348.
20 Christine de Pizan et al., *The Debate of the Romance of the Rose*,
   ed. and trans. David Hult (London, 2010), p. 60.
21 Christine de Pizan et al., *Le Débat sur le 'Roman de la rose'*,
   ed. and trans. Eric Hicks (Paris, 1977), p. 100. Translation my own.
22 Ibid., p. 9.
23 Ibid., pp. 11–12.
24 Ibid., p. 153.
25 Ibid., p. 12.
26 Christine often displays a mixture of humility and pride,
   a trait that Jacqueline Cerquiglini-Toulet has termed Christine's
   'orgueil humble' ('humble pride'): *La Couleur de la mélancolie:
   La Fréquentation des livres au XIVe siècle, 1300–1415* (Paris, 1993),
   p. 77.
27 Christine de Pizan et al., *Débat*, p. 12.
28 Ibid., pp. 18 and 20–21.
29 Ibid., p. 18.
30 Ibid., p. 19.
31 Ibid., p. 18.
32 *Romance of the Rose*, ed. and trans. Dahlberg, p. 113.
33 Ibid., p. 133.
34 Ibid., p. 135.
35 Renate Blumenfeld-Kosinski, ed., *Selected Writings*, p. 42.
36 Ibid.
37 Adapted from Christine de Pizan et al., *Poems of Cupid, God of
   Love: Christine de Pizan's 'Epistre au dieu d'amours' and 'Dit de la*

rose'; *Thomas Hoccleve's 'The Letter of Cupid'*, ed. and trans. Mary Carpenter Erler and Thelma S. Fenster (Leiden and New York, 1990), p. 113.

38 Ibid., p. 99.

39 Ibid., p. 105.

40 Translation adapted from *Romance of the Rose*, ed. and trans. Dahlberg, p. 31.

41 Christine de Pizan et al., *Poems of Cupid*, p. 101.

42 Ibid., p. 103.

43 Translation adapted from *Romance of the Rose*, ed. and trans. Dahlberg, p. 31. In Old French, the two opening lines read: 'Maintes genz cuident qu'en songe / N'ait se fable non et mençonge' – *Le Roman de la rose*, ed. Strubel, ll. 1–2.

44 On this, see Noah D. Guynn, 'Le Roman de la rose', in *The Cambridge Companion to Medieval French Literature*, ed. Simon Gaunt and Sarah Kay (Cambridge, 2008), pp. 48–62.

45 Christine de Pizan et al., *Poems of Cupid*, p. 119. In Old French, the lines read: 'Si me pensay que c'estoit songe. / Mais ne le tins pas a mençonge', ibid., p. 118.

46 Ibid., pp. 35–7.

47 Ibid., pp. 39–41.

48 Ibid., pp. 47–9.

49 'Je n'i fais riens fors reciter' ('I am doing nothing but reciting others') – *Le Roman de la rose*, ed. Strubel, l. 15238.

4 Christine's Legacy in Early Modern and Modern Culture

1 Christine de Pizan, *The Book of the City of Ladies and Other Writings*, ed. Sophie Bourgault and Rebecca Kingston, trans. Ineke Hardy (Cambridge, 2018), p. 27.

2 Seb Falk's *The Light Ages* (London, 2020) sets about correcting this view.

3 Martin le Franc, *Le Champion des dames*, 5 vols, ed. Robert Deschaux (Paris, 1999), vol. III, ll. 18953–60. Translation mine. Although Martin celebrates Christine for her Latin writings, only French texts survive. Whether or not she read Latin remains a point of debate.

4 Christine de Pizan et al., *Poems of Cupid, God of Love: Christine de Pizan's 'Epistre au dieu d'amours' and 'Dit de la rose'; Thomas Hoccleve's 'The Letter of Cupid'*, ed. and trans. Mary Carpenter Erler and Thelma S. Fenster (Leiden, 1990), pp. 159–60. As seen in

Chapter Three, such practices were common in the Middle Ages and not considered plagiarism as they might be today.

5 Christine de Pizan, *The Book of Deeds of Arms and of Chivalry*, trans. Sumner Willard, ed. Charity Cannon Willard (University Park, PA, 1999), p. 1.

6 See Rosalind Brown-Grant, 'Illumination as Reception: Jean Miélot's Reworking of the *Epistre Othea*', in *The City of Scholars: New Approaches to Christine de Pizan*, ed. Margarete Zimmerman and Dina de Rentiis (Berlin, 1994), pp. 260–71.

7 Everett L. Wheeler, 'Christine de Pizan's *Livre des fais d'armes et de chevalerie*: Gender and the Prefaces', *Nottingham Medieval Studies*, XLVI (2002), pp. 119–61 (pp. 124 and 133).

8 Voltaire, *Essai sur les mœurs et l'esprit des nations*, ed. René Pomeau (Paris, 1963), vol. I, p. 774.

9 Quoted in P.G.C. Campbell, 'Christine de Pisan en Angleterre', *Revue de littérature comparée*, V (1925), pp. 659–70 (p. 669). I have modernized the Old English.

10 Jennifer Summit, *Lost Property: The Woman Writer and English Literary History, 1380–1589* (London, 2000), p. 75.

11 Earl Jeffrey Richards, 'The Medieval "femme auteur" as a Provocation to Literary History: Eighteenth-century Readers of Christine de Pizan', in *The Reception of Christine de Pizan from the Fifteenth through the Nineteenth Centuries: Visitors to the City*, ed. Glenda McLeod (Lewiston, NY, 1991), pp. 101–32.

12 Ibid., pp. 106–7.

13 Jean-Marie-Louis Coupé, 'Anecdotes sur Christine de Pisan, ses romans et principaux ouvrages', *Bibliothèque Universelle des Romans*, II (1779), pp. 117–73 (p. 121). Translations from Coupé are all my own.

14 Ibid., p. 125.

15 Ibid., p. 128.

16 J. C. Laidlaw, 'Christine de Pizan, the Earl of Salisbury and Henry IV', *French Studies*, XXXVI (1982), pp. 129–43.

17 Richards, 'Femme auteur', pp. 120–21.

18 Simone de Beauvoir, *The Second Sex* (London, 1993), p. 111.

19 The article in question is William Minto, 'Christine de Pisan: A Medieval Champion of Her Sex', *Macmillan's Magazine*, LIII (1886), pp. 264–75.

20 Christine de Pizan, *The Treasure of the City of Ladies; or, The Book of the Three Virtues*, ed. Sarah Lawson (Harmondsworth, 1985), p. 62.

21 Ibid., p. 64.

22 Ibid., p. 63.

23 Sheila Delany, '"Mothers to Think Back Through": Who are They? The Ambiguous Example of Christine de Pizan', in *Medieval Literary Politics: Shapes of Ideology* (Manchester, 1990), pp. 88–103, p. 91.

24 See, for example, the discussion of prostitutes in Chapter One.

25 As pointed out in Christine M. Reno's rebuttal of Delany's piece in 'Christine de Pizan: At Best a Contradictory Figure?', in *Politics, Gender and Genre: The Political Thought of Christine de Pizan,* ed. Margaret Brabant (Oxford, 1992), pp. 171–91.

26 BBC Radio, 'Christine de Pizan: The Book of the City of Ladies', www.bbc.co.uk, accessed 3 July 2021.

27 Silvia Ballestra, *Christine e la città delle dame*, illus. Rita Petruccioli (Rome, 2015).

28 Barbara K. Altmann, 'Christine de Pizan: First Lady of the Middle Ages', in *Contexts and Continuities: Proceedings of the IVth International Colloquium on Christine de Pizan, Glasgow, 21–7 July 2000, published in honour of Liliane Dulac*, ed. Angus J. Kennedy and Liliane Dulac (Glasgow, 2002), vol. 1, pp. 17–30 (p. 27).

29 Details of editions of all of Christine's texts can be found at www.arlima.net.

30 Gustave Lanson, *Histoire de la littérature française* (Paris, 1955), pp. 166–6. Translation my own.

31 For examples, see @rebel_women_embroidery, @hiowbeorht, @dodwinb, @astrolettres.

32 Altmann, 'First Lady', p. 26.

33 Further details about *The Dinner Party* can be found in Judy Chicago, *The Dinner Party: From Creation to Preservation* (London, 2007).

34 Judy Chicago, *The Dinner Party: A Symbol of Our Heritage* (Garden City, NY, 1979), p. 79.

35 Chicago, *Preservation*, p. 136.

36 Ibid.

37 Chicago, *Heritage*, p. 13.

38 All of the collages that make up *Dinner in the City* can be viewed at Marsha Pippenger, 'Dinner in the City', https://pippengerart.com.

39 Ibid.

40 Turner Contemporary, 'Turner Prize 2019 Nominee, Tai Shani', www.youtube.com, 4 October 2019.

41 The monologues are published as Tai Shani, *Our Fatal Magic*
   (London, 2019).
42 Christine de Pizan, *City of Ladies*, ed. Bourgault and Kingston,
   p. 50.
43 Ibid., p. 31.
44 DACS, 'Tai Shani in Conversation', www.dacs.org.uk, 4 October
   2019.
45 Details of the *City of Ladies* installation are available from
   Domobaal gallery; see 'Exhibitions' at https://domobaal.com.
   There are plans for the video to be uploaded to an online space.

Conclusion

1 Christine de Pizan, *The Treasure of the City of Ladies; or, The Book
   of the Three Virtues*, ed. Sarah Lawson (Harmondsworth, 1985),
   p. 55.

LIST OF CHRISTINE DE PIZAN'S PRINCIPAL WORKS

Collections of Lyric Poetry

Les Cent balades (c. 1394–9)
Les Jeux a vendre (c. 1399–1402)
Autres balades (c. 1402–10)
Les Cent balades d'amant et de dame (c. 1402–10)
Les Complaintes amoureuses (c. 1402–10)

Devotional, Didactic and Moral Poetry

Les Enseignements moraux (c. 1398)
La Passion de Jhesu nostre sauveur (1398)
Les Proverbes moraux (c. 1400–1401)
L'Oroyson Nostre Dame (c. 1402–3)
Les Heures de contemplation de la Passion (1420)

Pro-feminine Works (poetry and prose)

L'Epistre au dieu d'amours (1399)
Le Dit de la rose (1401)
Les Epistres sur le Rommant de la rose (1401)
Le Livre de la cité des dames (c. 1405)
Le Livre du duc des vrais amans (c. 1404–5)
Le Livre des trois vertus (1405)

Autobiographical Narratives

Le Livre du chemin de longue estude (c. 1402–3)
Le Livre de la mutacion de Fortune (1403)
Le Livre de l'avision Christine (1405)

Political Works

Le Livre des fais et bonnes meurs du sage roy Charles v (1404)
L'Epistre a la reine de France (1405)

Le Livre du corps de policie (c. 1406–7)
Les Lamentacions sur les maux de la France (1410)
Le Livre des fais d'armes et de chevalerie (1410)
Le Livre de la paix (1414)
L'Epistre de la prison de vie humaine (c. 1416–18)
Le Ditié Jehanne d'Arc (1429)

Other Works

Le Dit de Poissy (1400)
L'Epistre Othea (c. 1400–1401)

SELECT BIBLIOGRAPHY

Manuscripts

'The Queen's Manuscript', London, British Library, Harley MS 4431, can be viewed online, www.bl.uk

The collection of Christine's manuscripts held at the Bibliothèque Nationale de France in Paris can be viewed at https://gallica.bnf.fr

French Editions of Christine's Texts

Ballades, Rondeaux, and Virelays: An Anthology, ed. Kenneth Varty (Leicester, 1965)

Le Chemin de longue étude, ed. Andrea Tarnowski (Paris, 2002)

Le Débat sur 'Le Roman de la rose', ed. Eric Hicks (Geneva, 1977)

Ditié de Jehanne d'Arc, ed. Angus J. Kennedy and Kenneth Varty (Oxford, 1977)

Epistre Othea, ed. Gabriella Parussa (Geneva, 1999)

Le Livre de l'advision Cristine, ed. Christine Reno and Liliane Dulac (Geneva, 2001)

Le Livre de la cité des dames (La città delle dame), ed. Patrizia Caraffi and Earl Jeffrey Richards (Milan, 1997)

Le Livre de la mutacion de Fortune, 4 vols, ed. Suzanne Solente (Paris, 1959–66)

Le Livre des fais et bonnes meurs du sage roy Charles V, 2 vols, ed. Susan Solente (Paris, 1936–40)

Le Livre des trois vertus, ed. Charity Cannon Willard and Eric Hicks (Paris, 1989)

Le Livre du corps de policie, ed. Angus J. Kennedy (Geneva, 1998)

Le Livre du Duc des vrais amants, ed. Thelma S. Fenster (Binghamton, NY, 1995)

Œuvres poétiques de Christine de Pizan, 3 vols, ed. Maurice Roy (Paris, 1886–96)

English Translations of Christine's Texts

The Book of the City of Ladies and Other Writings, ed. Sophie
    Bourgault and Rebecca Kingston, trans. Ineke Hardy
    (Cambridge, 2018)
The Book of Deeds of Arms and of Chivalry, trans. Sumner Willard,
    ed. Charity Cannon Willard (University Park, PA, 1999)
The Book of the Duke of True Lovers, ed. and trans. Thelma
    S. Fenster and Nadia Margolis (New York, 1991)
The Book of Peace, ed. Karen Green et al. (Pennsylvania, PA, 2008)
Christine's Vision, ed. and trans. Glenda McLeod (London, 1993)
The Debate of the Romance of the Rose, ed. and trans. David Hult
    (London, 2010)
'*The Epistle of the Prison of Human Life*' with '*An Epistle to the Queen
    of France*' and '*Lament on the Evils of the Civil War*', ed. and trans.
    Josette Wisman (New York, 1984)
*The Love Debate Poems of Christine de Pizan: 'Le Livre du debat de deux
    amans', 'Le Livre des trois jugemens', 'Le Livre du dit de Poissy'*,
    ed. Barbara K. Altmann (Gainesville, FL, 1998)
Othea's Letter to Hector, ed. and trans. Renate Blumenfeld-Kosinski
    and Earl Jeffrey Richards (Toronto, 2017)
*Poems of Cupid, God of Love: Christine de Pizan's 'Epistre au dieu
    d'amours' and 'Dit de la rose'; Thomas Hoccleve's 'The Letter
    of Cupid'*, ed. and trans. Mary Carpenter Erler and Thelma
    S. Fenster (Leiden and New York, 1990)
The Selected Writings of Christine de Pizan, ed. Renate Blumenfeld-
    Kosinski, trans. Renate Blumenfeld-Kosinski and Kevin
    Brownlee (New York and London, 1997)
The Treasure of the City of Ladies; or, The Book of the Three Virtues,
    ed. Sarah Lawson (Harmondsworth, 1985)

Studies on Christine de Pizan

Adams, Tracy, *Christine de Pizan and the Fight for France*
    (University Park, PA, 2014)
Altmann, Barbara K., and Deborah L. McGrady, eds, *Christine
    de Pizan: A Casebook* (New York, 2003)
Autrand, Françoise, *Christine de Pizan: Une femme en politique*
    (Paris, 2009)
Brabant, Margaret, ed., *Politics, Gender and Genre: The Political
    Thought of Christine de Pizan* (Oxford, 1992)

Brown-Grant, Rosalind, *Christine de Pizan and the Moral Defence of Women: Reading beyond Gender* (Cambridge, 1999)

Campbell, John, and Nadia Margolis, eds, *Christine de Pizan 2000: Studies of Christine de Pizan in Honour of Angus J. Kennedy* (Amsterdam, 2000)

Delany, Sheila, '"Mothers to Think Back Through": Who Are They? The Ambiguous Example of Christine de Pizan', in *Medieval Literary Politics: Shapes of Ideology* (Manchester, 1990), pp. 88–103

Demartini, Dominique, et al., eds, *Une femme de guerre à la fin du Moyen Âge: 'Le Livre des fais d'armes et de chevalerie' de Christine de Pizan* (Paris, 2016)

Desmond, Marilynn, ed., *Christine de Pizan and the Categories of Difference* (Minneapolis, MN, 1998)

Dor, Juliette, et al., eds, *Christine de Pizan: Une femme de science, une femme de lettres* (Paris, 2008)

Dulac, Liliane, and Bernard Ribémont, eds, *Une Femme de lettres au Moyen Âge: Études autour de Christine de Pizan* (Orleans, 1995)

Green, Karen, 'Was Christine de Pizan at Poissy 1418–1429?', *Medium Aevum*, LXIII/1 (2014), pp. 28–40

Hindman, Sandra, *Christine de Pizan's 'Epistre Othea': Painting and Politics at the Court of Charles VI* (Wetteren, 1986)

Kennedy, Angus J., et al., eds, *Contexts and Continuities: Proceedings of the IVth International Colloquium on Christine de Pizan (Glasgow, 21–7 July 2000). Published in Honour of Liliane Dulac*, 3 vols (Glasgow, 2002)

Laidlaw, J. C., 'Christine de Pizan: An Author's Progress', *Modern Language Review*, LXXVIII (1983), pp. 532–50

—, 'Christine de Pizan: A Publisher's Progress', *Modern Language Review*, LXXXII (1987), pp. 35–75

McLeod, Glenda K., ed., *The Reception of Christine de Pizan from the Fifteenth through the Nineteenth Centuries: Visitors to the City* (Lewiston, NY, 1991)

Margolis, Nadia, *An Introduction to Christine de Pizan* (Gainesville, FL, 2011)

Ouy, Gilbert, et al., *Album Christine de Pizan* (Turnhout, 2012)

Pinet, Marie-Josèphe, *Christine de Pisan, 1364–1430: Étude biographique et littéraire* (Paris, 1927)

Richards, Earl Jeffrey, *Christine de Pizan and Medieval French Lyric* (London, 1998)

—, ed., *Reinterpreting Christine de Pizan* (London, 1992)

Roux, Simone, *Christine de Pizan: Femme de tête, dame de cœur* (Paris, 2006)

Tarnowski, Andrea, ed., *Approaches to Teaching the Works of Christine de Pizan* (New York, 2018)

Willard, Charity Cannon, *Christine de Pizan: Her Life and Works* (New York, 1982)

Zimmerman, Margarete, and Dina de Rentiis, eds, *The City of Scholars: New Approaches to Christine de Pizan* (Berlin, 1994)

Studies on Medieval Culture and Literature

Adams, Tracy, *The Life and Afterlife of Isabeau of Bavaria* (Baltimore, MD, 2010)

Armstrong, Adrian, *The Virtuoso Circle: Competition, Collaboration, and Complexity in Late Medieval French Poetry* (Tempe, AZ, 2012)

—, and Sarah Kay, *Knowing Poetry: Verse in Medieval France from the Rose to the Rhétoriqueurs* (London, 2011)

Autrand, Françoise, *Charles v: Le Sage* (Paris, 1994)

Bouchet, Florence, *Le Discours sur la lecture en France aux XIVe et XVe siècles: Pratiques, poétique, imaginaire* (Paris, 2008)

Bove, Boris, and Claude Girard, eds, *Le Paris du Moyen Âge* (Paris, 2018)

Brown, Cynthia J., *Poets, Patrons and Printers: Crisis of Authority in Late Medieval France* (London, 1995)

Brownlee, Kevin, and Sylvia Huot, eds, *Rethinking the Romance of the Rose: Text, Image, Reception* (Philadelphia, PA, 1992)

Cayley, E. J., *Debate and Dialogue: Alain Chartier in His Cultural Context* (Oxford, 2006)

Cerquiglini-Toulet, Jacqueline, *La Couleur de la mélancolie: La Fréquentation des livres au XIVe siècle, 1300–1415* (Paris, 1993), translated as *The Colour of Melancholy*, trans. Lydia G. Cochrane (London, 1997)

Clanchy, Michael T., *From Memory to Written Record: England, 1066–1307* (Oxford and Malden, 2013)

Croenen, Godfried, and Peter F. Ainsworth, eds, *Patrons, Authors and Workshops: Books and Book Production in Paris around 1400* (Louvain, 2006)

Delsaux, Olivier, *Manuscrits et pratiques autographes chez les écrivains français de la fin du Moyen Âge: L'Exemple de Christine de Pizan* (Geneva, 2013)

Falk, Seb, *The Light Ages* (London, 2020)

Fiero, Gloria K., et al., eds, *Three Medieval Views of Women: La Contenance des fames, Le Bien des fames, Le Blasme des fames* (New Haven, CT, 1989)

Gaunt, Simon, and Sarah Kay, eds, *The Cambridge Companion to Medieval French Literature* (Cambridge, 2008)

Kay, Sarah, *The Place of Thought: The Complexity of One in Late Medieval French Didactic Poetry* (Philadelphia, PA, 2008)

Leyser, Henrietta, *Medieval Women: A Social History of Women in England, 450–1500* (London, 1995)

Looze, Laurence de, *Pseudo-autobiography in the Fourteenth Century: Juan Ruiz, Guillaume de Machaut, Jean Froissart and Geoffrey Chaucer* (Gainesville, FL, 1997)

Lorentz, Philippe, and Dany Sandron, *Atlas de Paris au Moyen Âge: Espace urbain, habitat, société, religion, lieux de pouvoir* (Paris, 2006)

McGrady, Deborah, *The Writer's Gift or the Patron's Pleasure? The Literary Economy in Late Medieval France* (Toronto, 2019)

McWebb, Christine, and Earl Jeffrey Richards, eds, *Debating the 'Roman de la rose': A Critical Anthology* (London, 2007)

Meiss, Millard, *French Painting in the Time of Jean de Berry: The Late Fourteenth Century and the Patronage of the Duke* (London, 1967)

Musée du Louvre, *Paris 1400: Les Arts sous Charles VI* (Paris, 2004)

Solterer, Helen, *The Master and Minerva: Disputing Women in French Medieval Culture* (Berkeley, CA, 1995)

Summit, Jennifer, *Lost Property: The Woman Writer and English Literary History, 1380–1589* (London, 2000)

Swift, Helen J., *Gender, Writing, and Performance: Men Defending Women in Late Medieval France, 1440–1538* (Oxford, 2008)

Taylor, Jane, *The Making of Poetry: Late Medieval French Poetic Anthologies* (Turnhout, 2007)

—, and Lesley Smith, eds, *Women and the Book: Assessing the Visual Evidence* (London, 1997)

ACKNOWLEDGEMENTS

In 2016, when working in the Cambridge University Library, a fellow reader remarked on the hefty tome lying open on the desk next to me, a copy of the *Album Christine de Pizan*. From across the desk, he commented that he had once worked on Christine himself, 'her images, mind you, not her texts', he said. I excitedly replied that I was in the process of putting the finishing touches to my PhD thesis, which was precisely on the subject of text–image relations in Christine's works, and suggested we talk further. This encounter with the reader, who turned out to be Professor Nigel Morgan, Honorary Professor of the History of Art at Corpus Christi College, Cambridge, was one of a series of fortuitous encounters without which this book would not exist.

A few months later, when I was invited to present my research at a seminar in Cambridge, I contacted Nigel and invited him to come along. He brought with him an art historian from the Fitzwilliam Museum named Dr Deirdre Jackson, with whom I have since shared many enjoyable conversations about Christine and medieval visual culture in general. Deirdre mentioned that she had been tasked with suggesting writers for a new series on medieval lives to Reaktion Books, for which she thought a title on Christine would make an excellent contribution. Thinking that she was meaning to tell me that she was herself to write this volume, I was disappointed that the opportunity to write a book on Christine aimed at a general audience had passed me by. This feeling was short-lived, as I soon realized she was in fact suggesting I should be the one to write it. A few weeks later, I was in touch with Michael Leaman at Reaktion, who has since been tremendously patient with me while the project took shape. And so, as a result of that big book lying open on the desk next to me, my own little book has been born.

Deirdre, Nigel and Michael are foremost among the people who have helped bring about the publication of this book, as are the rest of the team at Reaktion – in particular, Alex Ciobanu and Phoebe Colley. For assistance with the historical content of the book, thanks are due to Savannah Pine for providing helpful details on Charles v's library and the ritual brotherhood of Louis of Orleans and his uncle, and to Malek Karataş for her information on sworn illuminators in fourteenth-century

Paris. Julie Summers, a fellow of the Royal Literary Fund based out of St Hilda's College in Oxford during the 2019–2020 academic year, offered excellent and reassuring suggestions on writing for a popular audience. Without her advice, I have no doubt this book would have been much less appealing to the audiences for whom it is intended. Penelope Haralambidou treated me to a wonderful and very memorable guided tour of her artwork, for which I am enormously grateful, as did Marsha Pippenger, whom I had the great pleasure of meeting at the Christine de Pizan colloquium in Louvain-la-Neuve in 2015. I trust my enthusiasm for both projects comes across in these pages. As readers, Martin Cole, Peter Cooper-Davis, Coby Goodchild, Jon Hawes and Katie Nolan offered further valuable improvements and suggestions that have also helped to make this book more accessible. I am thankful both for their comments and for the interest they have since shown in Christine. Additional thanks go to Shay Hamias for the map of fifteenth-century Paris that he produced for this book, and to Pete for his technical assistance with the graphics in these pages. I also extend my gratitude to the librarians at the Bodleian, St Hilda's College, the Taylor Institution and Weston Libraries in Oxford, and the staff at the University Library in Cambridge. I am especially grateful to the Oxford libraries for their help in making resources available via the Emergency Temporary Access Service during the global pandemic, without which it would have been impossible to finish writing this book. Particular thanks are owed to Nick Hearn for providing invaluable support. Over the course of this project, I am grateful to have had the opportunity to teach some dazzling students at St Hilda's College and the University of Oxford more widely, whose enthusiasm for Christine has spurred me on through difficult times. I sincerely hope Christine will stay with them as she has with me.

And finally, to members of my family and my dear friends – Jane, Ben, Sophie, Emilia, Alison, Ronnie, Margaret, Alex, Karl and Jane, members of 'The Chaucers' and of 'The Caledonian Odyssey' – for putting up with my anecdotes about medieval Paris and endless fascination with Christine that has endured for well over a decade. I hope this book will demonstrate why my obsession shows no sign of abating.

PHOTO ACKNOWLEDGEMENTS

The author and publishers wish to express their thanks to the below sources of illustrative material and/or permission to reproduce it. Every effort has been made to contact copyright holders; should there be any we have been unable to reach or to whom inaccurate acknowledgements have been made please contact the publishers, and full adjustments will be made to any subsequent printings. Some locations of artworks are also given below, in the interest of brevity:

Courtesy of the Amis de la Tour Jean-sans-Peur: p. 30; Biblioteca Histórica, Universitat de València: pp. 96 (MS 387, fol. 145v), 100 (MS 387, fol. 147v); Bibliothèque de l'Arsenal, Paris: p. 120 (MS 5073, fol. 211v); Bibliothèque nationale de France (BNF), Paris: pp. 22 (MS fr. 24287, fol. 2r), 32 (MS fr. 23279, fol. 119r), 58 (MS fr. 25526, fol. 77v), 66 (MS fr. 1176, fol. 17v), 73 (MS fr. 1643, fol. 1r), 84 (MS fr. 603, fol. 49r); © Bibliothèque royale de Belgique (KBR), Brussels: pp. 38 (MS 10982, fol. 2r), 124 (MS 4373-76, fol. 56v); © Bodleian Libraries, University of Oxford (CC BY-NC 4.0): p. 108 (MS Douce 195, fol. 76v); Boston Public Library, MA: p. 68 (MS fr. Med. 101, fol. 32v); © British Library Board, all rights reserved/Bridgeman Images: pp. 6 (Harley MS 4431, fol. 129r), 46 (Harley MS 4380, fol. 1r), 77 (Harley MS 4431, fol. 259v), 90 (Harley MS 4431, fol. 290r); © 2021 Judy Chicago/Artists Rights Society (ARS), New York/DACS, London, photo courtesy of Judy Chicago/Art Resource, NY (photo © Donald Woodman): p. 144; courtesy Peter Cooper-Davis and Shay Hamias: pp. 34–5; © Camilla Falsini, courtesy of Lavazza and the artist: p. 140; © Penelope Haralambidou, courtesy of the artist (photo Charlotte Cooper-Davis): p. 153; © Koei Tecmo/Omega Force: p. 136; Musée Condé, Chantilly: p. 29 (MS 65, fol. 10v); © 2007 Marsha Monroe Pippenger, photos courtesy of the artist: pp. 146, 147.

INDEX

Illustration numbers are indicated by *italics*